gourmet food with all of the flavor and none of the guilt

THE GUILT FREE GOURMET

Low Calorie, Low Fat Cooking Guide: 2023
COOKBOOK VOLUME 1
Fourth Edition

Follow me online at:

The Web: www.theguiltfreegourmet.net
Connect: @dhallakx7
Facebook: The Guilt Free Gourmet LLC.
Instagram: TheGuiltFreeGourmet ... No, seriously... Follow me on Instagram.
Youtube Channel: The Guilt Free Gourmet
You can find this book, as well as all my Cookbooks, on Amazon.com
(not to be confused with that old vegan, gluten free, hippie dessert book of the same name... That's not mine)
Amazon: Leave a book review, or I'll figure out a way to get coal in your stocking.

LEGAL MUMBO JUMBO

The Guilt Free Gourmet® 2022-23

Weight Watchers International & WW ®

This publication is dedicated to my loving wife, whom I will never deserve. You have stood by me, a steadfast rock, weathering every storm and tempest that we've faced. You have supported and encouraged me during every phase of the past 18 years, and have held my hand through the darkest nights. Thank you for saying "Yes" all those years ago and for putting up with me ever since. On a positive, at least there's a whole lot less of me for you to put up with now.

- Daniel

Is This A Cookbook?

Yes... and No. When I published the first edition of this cooking guide, back in December 2018, it was born out of a desire to try and help absolutely every single person in-program that I could. Every single day I'd log into Connect and read about people struggling, not knowing how to work the system, or unaware of all of the awesome little tips and tricks that we all use in our food prep. I thought that it would be a tremendous service, if I could try and compile all the food hacks and cooking cheats that I'd learned about, then put them into one place.

The original Cooking Guide that I published in 2018 had such an overwhelming response. I never would have imagined that there was such an insane desire and need for something like this. All of the famous food bloggers and chefs... they all pump out cookbooks like a conveyor belt. Here's the thing though... ever heard that age-old adage, "Give a man a fish and you feed him for a day. Teach him to fish and you feed him for life."? Well... same principle. My entire purpose for writing and putting this together is to <u>TEACH YOU</u> to cook differently, on your own, without me. I don't want to teach you to just blindly follow my recipes. I want to SHOW YOU how to use my basic principles to get those gears turning in your head, so that you have the light switch turn on and YOU start hacking down regular recipes like I do. I want to embolden you, and get you to start thinking outside of the box, with recipes and ingredients on your own.

I want you to finish reading through this cooking guide and feel empowered in your kitchen. I want you to try out new techniques and ingredients that you wouldn't have before. I want you to close this baby, open up the Recipe Builder and start playing around with modifying recipes, like a rockstar. Between my Foundation recipes and the low point sauce recipes, combined with the pages of food hack and ingredient swap ideas... you should be able to look at almost ANY recipe, from any website or magazine, then start dropping points like Godzilla drops skyscrapers in Tokyo.

<u>HOW MANY POINTS PER SERVING ARE YOUR RECIPES?</u>

For this newly revised version of my cookbook, for the 2023 plan, I'll be providing point values in 2 ways. Traditional AND a QR code you can scan. In this example, under 'points', you'll see a blue text bubble with 2 numbers. The **LEFT** number is points on the 'regular' plan, while the **RIGHT** number is the point value for the diabetic plan. Easy peasy.

R = Regular 0 point foods list
D = Diabetic 0 point foods list

R   D

0-1

So in this case, the first serving is 0 points for folks on the 'regular' plan and 1 point for people on the 'diabetic' plan.

What The Heck Are These Weird Lookin' Square Thingies??

For those of you who are what we'd call 'old school', these things are known as a '***QR Code***'. QR meaning '***Quick Response***' code. They act like a barcode you'd see on the side of a product at the store. The difference being, THESE are used to act as a 'link'. Look at one of these with your phone's camera app, and just like clicking on a text-link on a website... these open up a new browser on your mobile device and take you somewhere, or show you something.

I go into more detail on how they'll be used in this book, on page 10. But suffice to say, if you want to find the accurate 'point' information for your specific plan Go ahead and check out page 10, then come back here and try scanning this baby. Consider it a test... a test where, if you get it right, you get to hang out with me and *@chiafullo*, in Lederhosen.

Table of Contents

2023 | Cookbook: Volume 1
Low Calorie, Low Fat Cooking Strategies, Guides & Recipes

Introduction

How To Scan QR Codes

Important Kitchen Gadgets

Ingredient Swaps & Substitutions

Recipe Builder Tutorial

Eggs Benedict with Low Calorie Hollandaise & Smoked Salmon

Fresh, Home Made Pasta, with White Wine Butter Garlic Sauce

Foundation Recipes

Meat Seasoning Mixes

Sauces

Closing Thoughts & Acknowledgements

Nutritional Info. & Macros

Recipe Index

Really? Free Cookbooks?

Though all of my cookbooks are available in printed format, on Amazon.com, you can open, view, save, print and share ALL of my cookbooks for free, at absolutely no charge whatsoever on my website: *www.theguiltfreegourmet.net*

I allow everyone access to my Cookbooks for free, in digital format. My website has no ads, promotions, pop ups, or links begging you to use my discount code and save 10% on something so I get a kickback. <u>This is my ministry</u>. Yeah, a coupla bucks is nice, but at the end of the day, the most important thing is feeling like I get to help people. For a guy who gave up his career to stay home and take care of two handicapped kiddos, this is my release. Making these cookbooks helps me out, just as much as it does you.

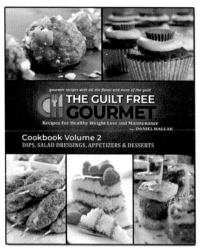

The Guilt Free Gourmet
<u>Cookbook Volume 2</u>
- Dips & Spreads
- Salad Dressings
- Gourmet Appetizers
- Cupcakes & Cakes

The Guilt Free Gourmet
<u>Cookbook Volume 3</u>
- Dressings, Spreads & Condiments
- Burgers, Sandwiches & Sausages
- Side Dishes
- Salads
- Bonus Recipes

The Guilt Free Gourmet
<u>Cookbook Volume 4</u>
- Salad Dressings
- Dips
- Holiday Side Dishes
- Holiday Desserts
(currently being revised for Fall '23)

The Guilt Free Gourmet
<u>Cookbook Volume 5</u>
- Sauces & Dips
- Dim Sum/Appetizers & Soups
- Regional entrees from:
    Cambodia, China, Korea, Japan,
    Thailand, Vietnam & Taiwan

Introduction

Alright, for you folks that already have "The 2019 Low Point Cooking Guide" or follow me on Connect, this is going to be preeeeetty repetitive. Sorry *shrugs* This is mainly for the folks that don't know me yet.

Hi there, my name is Daniel, but most of you know me from **WW Connect** as dhallakx7. As of the writing of this cookbook, I'm a 41-year-old stay at home dad to my 2 special needs kidlettes, Rachel (Autistic) and Jesse (Down Syndrome). Prior to this, I worked as a Graphic Designer & Web Developer for a really great company. I had just received a promotion, but when Jesse was born preemie and his diagnosis was finally confirmed, our priorities had to change, so I became Mr. Mom.

I still remember the night in 3rd grade when I turned from liking food, to wanting to gorge on food. My best friend Bart and I went to a high school soccer game with my older brother. At that game I saw something that I'd never seen before. A food vendor showed up in the bleachers pushing a food cart. He was using it to make hot, sugar coated mini cake donuts, fresh to order. I remember running down to that cart with my friend, looking at the fresh donuts, then immediately running up to my brother and asking for the money to buy some... then to buy some more... then to buy some more. And that's where it started.

I spent the better part of the next 30 years going from "husky" to overweight, eventually becoming heavy enough to be classified as obese. I only went swimming 3 or 4 times in the past 25 years out of shame for how I looked. I would make excuses not to see friends who were visiting from out of town, whom I hadn't seen in years. Heck, I wouldn't even change in the same room as my wife because I was

The new and improved 2019 Dad Bod GTO. Now available with dual child carriers, improved mileage and extended warranty.

embarrassed about my body. Yet, did it make me want to change and lose weight? Nope, I figured it wasn't worth it.

In order to lose weight, I was going to be eating nothing but rice cakes and tasteless diet food. I would have to start going to the gym, running and stop eating all the foods that I loved to eat. People on diets are always so miserable and complain about what they can't eat, how their diet de jour doesn't allow them to have sugar, or they are cutting all carbs, or they are doing "cleanses" or whatever insane dietary deprivation is the current trend. Why in the heck would I want to do that? I'd rather be fat and eating than be skinny and surviving on rice cakes, bean curd and sadness. But, when I finally hit my mental rock bottom, I stumbled upon an article online late at night. It was written by a female blogger who tried Weight Watchers for one month without doing any exercise and without giving up eating regular food. She ended up losing 5 pounds over the course of the month without working out, while still eating normal foods and staying within her Weight Watchers daily allotment of "Smart Points". I figured it was worth a shot as I had no

Don't let food manipulate you, learn to manipulate your food

Rethink How You Cook

- Lower the fat, calories, sugar and carbs of foods, by swapping out high fat & calorie ingredients.
- Lose weight, by turning high fat & calorie food that you love, into a leaner and healthier dish.
- Retrain your brain to automatically think of ingredient substitutions, making this journey livable, sustainable, and enjoyable with GREAT food.

Cont.

Introduction

desire to stop eating normal food and no desire to exercise (at that time). The first few weeks were difficult but manageable. I was losing weight, I wasn't working out, but dear Lord, there was so much food that I missed eating that I couldn't have because it was so high in points. Then it happened... I found the "recipe builder' tool, within the WW mobile phone App, that pretty much changed everything.

I immediately realized the full possibilities the tool offered. I bought a cooking magazine from the grocery store, that had a recipe on the cover for a skillet full of baked rolls covered in tons of cheese, marinara sauce, pepperoni and Italian sausage. The type of meal there is NO WAY you could ever eat on Weight Watchers and stay within your points.

I scoured Connect for ingredient swap ideas and even came up with a few ideas of my own. I started swapping out regular cheese for fat free cheese and mixed in some plain yogurt for added creaminess. I adjusted spice amounts, checked how much wine I could cut with water to reduce the points and still taste it in a sauce. I tried getting as creative as I possibly could to make the skillet as low fat and low calorie as possible. Each time I did that with a new recipe, it became more and more fun, like challenging myself to solve a difficult puzzle. Now I can look at almost any recipe and think of ways to almost immediately start cutting the calories, while retaining the flavor.

Now, I absolutely LOVE doing this. I wake up every day, genuinely looking forward to "what am I going to try and make today?" I love logging in to the WW mobile app to check and see if there's anyone that needs a question answered, or needs help with a recipe... I love getting tagged by people who are looking for help.

After being stuck in a house, changing diapers, vacuuming, or being a taxi all day... getting to interact with adults who value you and want to chat, even if it's digitally, is such a relief.

Using QR Codes

Have you ever seen those crazy looking, square shaped code-thingies on a menu, flier or in a magazine and wondered what they are? Well... they are the exact same as a 'link' you'd find on a webpage, which you can click to go somewhere. But, these links are printed onto paper. You use a mobile device's Camera to scan (click) them.

So you don't have to "take my word for it", with my listed recipe's points, I wanted to provide you a way to check them for yourself, while also giving you the ability to track them. For all my recipes, if you scan the codes in this book, you'll be taken to my website, where you can click a link for any dish. That link will open up my recipe in YOUR app's recipe builder. This will let you see the accurate points on your plan, AS WELL AS LETTING YOU TRACK what you ate!

Step One:

Open your phone's "camera" app, ya'know, the one you take pictures with. Open it, then point the camera at the square code-thingie you want to look up.

Step Two:

When you see 4 little yellow brackets around the corners of the code you want, a pop up that says "*Open QR.IO in Safari*" will appear at the top of the screen.
Click that banner.

Step Three:

Once you click that banner, your device will open up the 'plan values' page on my website.

From there, scroll down, find the recipe you'd like point values for, then click the recipe's picture.

Step Four:

When you click the recipe's picture, it will instantly load up my recipe into YOUR WW app (if on a mobile device). If you're on a desktop, there's no need to scan a code. Just go to the 'Point Values' page on my site and click the recipe.

Your App will show you the points for my recipe, based off of YOUR 0 point food settings. Then, simply 'track' the food, adjust the servings, etc.

*** IMPORTANT ***

Once scanned, the links on my website will start up your WW app, showing you MY recipe, saved within the WW database. Sounds cool, right? Well... for bloggers and cookbook authors, this presents a legal grey area.

The WW App, the WW 'point' calculator and the WW database are all copyrighted by WW. Posting direct links on blogs or from cookbooks, directly TO the WW database maaaaay be construed as a breach of WW's Intellectual Property. As such, I have reached out to WW for clarification and asked if it would be possible to come to a licensing arrangement, so that I can link directly from my recipes in this cookbook, TO their App.

Until I am given permission, or some type of licensing arrangement can be made, my QR codes within this book will NOT link to my recipes in their database. Instead, scanning the QR codes in this cookbook, will instead take you to my 100% advertisement and revenue-free website, where you can find links to the recipe's point values. I apologize for the hopefully temporary inconvenience, but... legal's legal. Someday, the QR codes in this book will directly open up your app, but until that day... I have to use the website workaround. Sorry.

For most of you folks that cook a lot and have spent years trying new things in the kitchen, these Gadgets & Gizmos are nothing new to you. But this particular page is directed more towards people who aren't as comfortable in the kitchen yet and are wondering what some of the things are that I mention a lot in my posts. I've often heard people say "what's a food processor,?" or "Immersion Blender?" Well I thought it'd be a good use of a page to point out what some of the primary things are that I use, and what their purpose is, for the newer cooks in the kitchen.

1. Food Processor

Think of a food processor of a giant, wide bottomed blender. There are quite a few dips and dressings that are in this cookbook that rely heavily on using a food processor. ESPECIALLY the guacamole and the hummus. Sweet Lord in Heaven, it's worth it to get an inexpensive food processor for the Hummus recipe alone.

You don't need to buy an expensive model. Even just an inexpensive one from Big Lots will do the job. It is a necessity for a couple of the recipes.

2. Pasta Makers

Fresh pasta, if made the way that I teach, is lower in points and calories than store bought dried pasta. The Foundation recipe section has a great step by step tutorial for making fresh pasta. Making your pasta in the way that I show in this guide, will allow you to make a pasta sheet half the size of a sheet pan, for just 3 points.

3. Wire Strainers

These are used EXTENSIVELY in my cupcake and cake recipes, as well as in a few of the dips and sauces. You don't need an expensive set. I got mine at the 99 cent store and they've lasted for years.

4. Immersion Blender

YOU NEED THIS IN YOUR LIFE! It's essentially a small blender at the end of a stick. It is used in all of the recipes for my "creamy" dressings. Throw all of the dressing ingredients into the cup, use the immersion blender... you have dressing in 15 seconds. You can also use a regular blender as well, but it takes up a lot more counterspace. You can purchase an inexpensive one at walmart for $20. You don't need the ultra expensive brands that have more gadgets than a swiss army knife.

5. Stock Pot with Steamer Inserts

This sounds like something that would be crazy expensive, but I've seen them at Ross and Marshalls for $20-$30. They are so worth it. I use the deep insert to steam cakes inside of a Corningware ceramic round dish, as well as using it to steam my Weight Watchers friendly Tamales (in the 'featured recipes' on my website). I use the shallower steamer insert to steam 2 ingredient dough for Asian steamed buns, banh mi bites and stuffed tamaleball appetizers.
.There are crazy ridiculous big brand ones, but honestly, you can find a $40 one on Amazon that will last you forever.

You may be fighting the thought of that purchase, but once you make the tamales and steamed cake, you won't regret it.

Swaps, Hacks, & Tips

The Fat Free "cheese hack" lets you have melty cheese for an entire pan of Lasagna for only 4-5 total points

Crushed Bran Cereal Pie Crust

Low Point & Carb Breading

13 points of Fresh Pasta

13 points of Store Bought

Retrain Your Brain

If you think about it, the primary purpose of the Recipe Builder in the Weight Watchers App is to make us WANT to cook our food with less fat, calories, sugars and carbs. Every time you lower the point value of a recipe with ingredient swaps, you have cut 1 or all those 4 things.

Lowering the Points for Butter

Molly McButter Fat Free Sprinkles

This stuff is amazing. It's a fine powder that dissolves perfectly in liquids and gives the flavor and color of butter. You can use up to 1 tablespoon for 0 points. It's a go-to staple in my kitchen for sauces.

I Can't Believe It's Not Butter- Light

Don't get one of the other types of I Can't Believe It's Not Butter spreads. Make sure you get the one that says "Light" and scan it to make sure. It is a butter flavored spread that can be used perfectly in place of butter, but at a fraction of the points. A ¼ cup is only 6 points, while ¼ cup of real butter is 23 or 24, depending on brand. Perfect for when you MUST use butter, but need to reduce the points, calories, and fat.

ULTRA Low Point Pie Crusts

Kellogg's All-Bran or Fiber One

Traditionally, for a pie crust you'd use crushed up graham crackers. But the amount of graham crackers and butter for that is around 36-46 points. If you put All-Bran or Fiber One cereal in a food processor with a little bit of FF Yogurt and some 0 point sugar replacement and sugar free maple syrup, along with some I Can't Believe It's Not Butter Light, you can make an entire pie crust for only 7-10 points.

Yogurt For Oil In Cake Mixes

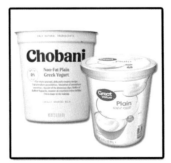

Fat Free Plain Greek Yogurt

Yogurt is a good substitute for mayo and sour cream in most recipes, though it can easily curdle when introduced into sauces or hot liquids. Let the liquids or dishes cool a bit before you bring the yogurts up to temperature and mix them in. Adding cornstarch helps with the curdling issues. You can also use Greek to make salad dressings instead of mayo.

Fat Free Plain Yogurt I personally prefer to use Plain Yogurt as a substitute for sour cream, rather than Greek Yogurt, as it is thinner and more closely resembles the viscosity of oil.

0 Point Sugar Free Jelly/Spread

But... It's So High In Points??

NOPE!!! Want about 2/3 cup of fruit spread for 0 points? Sugar Free smucker's jelly used to let you have 1 Tbsp for 0 points, but now the new system has taken it down to only letting you have 2 tsp for 0. So, let's make our own, in under 10 minutes. Simply heat up 1 cup of berries in a pot, with 1/4 cup water and 3 Tbsp 0 point sugar replacement. Once it breaks down, stir in 1-1/2 tsp cornstarch that's dissolved with 2 tsp water. Stir and let it boil for 3-4 minutes, till thickened. Done.

Sugar Free Syrup Instead of Honey

How To Swap Out Bee Puke.

As delicious and complex a flavor as honey is, it is also very high in points and sugars. My favorite sub. for honey, is cheap and easy to find... *Sugar Free Pancake Syrup.* The flavor profile is different, but it is sweet, thick and a lot lower in points. Unfortunately, under the 2023 plan, it's higher in points than before. You USED to be able to have a least 2-1/2 Tbsp of it for 0 points. Now, the generic listing only lets you have 1-7/8 Tbsp for 0. There are still a few brands that let you have more, but they are harder to come across for most folks. Regardless, using Sugar Free syrup is a great way to keep a sweet flavor in a sauce or dish, while cutting hundreds or even thousands of calories from the recipe.

Low Point Breading for Meats & Veggies

Non Traditional Breading Ideas

Store bought breadcrumbs pack a pretty high point punch. Want lower point bread crumbs? Try Mashed potato flakes, or crushed rice krispies, whole wheat cheerios, or corn flakes. There's also the obvious fix... buy low point bread, like Sara Lee 45 calorie, or 'Keto' 1 point slices, then make crumbs.

Melting Fat Free Cheese Hack

Fat Free Mozzarella & Cheddar

Using this hack you can "cheese" an entire pan of Lasagna with 3 cups of fat free mozzarella, with an extra 1 cup of Greek (4 total cups) for 4 points. The biggest problem with FF cheese is it doesn't melt. That's solved if you mix it with a bit of FF plain (or Greek) yogurt. Sounds wrong, but it's amazing. Mix any amount of Kraft (or other brand) Fat Free shredded cheese with about 3/4 as much FF plain yogurt and mix until it forms a cheesy goopy mixture. Use it on Chicken Parmesan, Lasagnas or stuffed in a chicken breast. It works like a charm.

Fresh Pasta to the Rescue

Don't Give Up Your Pasta!!!!

For most people who are on a 'diet', pasta is your sad emoji. Yes, there's store bought pasta that's crazy-high in carbs, calories and points... then there's homemade low point pasta! Rejoice! Using the recipe on pages 40-43, I'll show you how real, fresh pasta is lower in carbs, points and is easier to portion than store bought pasta. Not to mention it tastes 10,000 times better than that dried stuff you buy for $1.

99% Fat Free Bratwurst, Chorizo, & More

with Seasoned Ground Turkey

Don't get me wrong, I like beef... but ground beef is expensive, is high in points and sits in my gut like a brick. I've spent a LOT of time developing ground meat seasonings (pg's 26-31), that allow you to have low point, calorie and fat, chorizo, italian sausage, bratwurst and more. It's an incredibly tasty way to cut calories from your meals, without really losing much in the way of that dish's traditional flavor. Give the recipes a try, you won't regret it.

Quickly "Ripen" Yellow Bananas

Sweeten up those baked goods

Ever tried to make a banana bread or another baked item that calls for "very ripe" bananas, but all that you have are the firm yellow ones without a fleck of black on them? Here's a quick fix. Throw the firm bananas (in their skin) onto a pie pan, and bake them at 325 degrees for 15-20 minutes, then let it cool.

Pudding without Milk or Yogurt

Thickening without Dairy or Fat

It's one of the annoying things about pudding, it just won't thicken if you use water, soy milk, almond milk or whatever. Well, that's not the case. If you use HALF as much of a non fatty fluid as the directions call for milk, it works. If you want it to have the consistency of regular pudding, use 1 cup of COLD liquid in place of the 2 cups milk. If you are wanting it thick enough to where it can keep its shape for a frosting, use 2/3 cup. So, use (1) 1oz packet of instant pudding and 1 cup cold water for pudding or 3/4 to 2/3 cup for frosting.

Celery Root is actually a good substitute for french fries

Research Tirelessly

Other than telling you to dig into the Recipe Builder, this is the best advice I can give you on this food journey. When it comes to ideas for food substitutions, the Internet is your friend. Most of the things that I've thought to try came from late night Google searches, trying to figure out how I could substitute or make lower versions of things.

THINK OUTSIDE THE BOX!! I didn't reinvent the wheel with this stuff, I just pulled it from somewhere else and Weight Watcher-ized it. A prime example is the Low Point Pie Crust. I found the idea for that on a Diabetic cooking site because they have to drastically reduce their sugar intake. When I wanted to find 0sp potato alternatives for French fries, I figured that I should look on "low carb" cooking forums and sites. The goal of this system is to retrain us to make healthier food choices, and the goal of the recipe builder is to subtlety push us towards making our foods as healthy (and lower in points) as possible.

Challenge yourself to think. Find or try new ways to substitute ingredients. Then you'll be able to have pretty much anything, guilt free, with a little bit of time in the kitchen.

Potato Substitutes (depending on your 'plan')

0 Point Potato Alternatives

There are some of you folks that are going to cling to your potatoes being 0 points still... It's ok, you do you. But, for everyone else, I thought it'd point out a few root-ish veggies that, if used in the right way, can be viable substitutes for potatoes in different dishes. Some have similar flavors and textures, while others range from having an herby or a slightly sweet taste. All you can do is experiment and find what works best for you. My personal favorite is 'celery root'.

Rutabaga, Radish & Parsnips

Rutabaga is a root vegetable that falls into the same family as broccoli, brussel sprouts and kale. Once it's washed and peeled, a rutabaga's orange flesh is similar in texture and flavor to a turnip. As for Radish, you normally only see them as a raw garnish. In their raw form, they are bitter and spicy. However, when you cook them, they mellow out and take on a more potato-like texture. Parsnips are FANTASTIC. They taste like a cross between a carrot and a potato. However,... parsnips aren't 0 on all plans.

Celery Root (listed as "celeriac" in the App)

Celeriac has a mild celery flavor and is often used as a flavoring in soups and stews. It can also be used on its own, usually mashed, or used in casseroles, au gratins and baked dishes. It has a naturally savory flavor.

Jicama

Jicama resembles a large light-brown colored turnip. The white, creamy interior has a very crisp texture somewhat similar to a firm apple or raw potato. Cooking jicama or serving it raw are equally tasty ways to prepare this lightly sweet root

Pureed/Mashed Fruit & Veggies in Cake

More alternatives to oil in baking

As well as using fat free plain yogurt like we mentioned earlier, no sugar added and pureed fruits and vegetables are perfect 1:1 swaps in baking for most, if not all, of the recommended liquid ingredients listed on boxed cake mixes. Make sure to scan labels first though, as some brands DO add sugar.

DIY Self Rising Flour

Perfect for Gluten Free folks

Members with Gluten sensitivities have a rough time with a lot of recipes, especially the 2 ingredient dough that we all know and love. Simply add 1-1/2 teaspoons of baking powder and 1/4 teaspoon of salt to every 1 cup of WHATEVER flour you would like to use. Whether it's gluten free, whole wheat, cornmeal or any type of flour you want.

Also, I HIGHLY RECOMMEND 'Bob's Red Mill' 1 to 1 Baking Flour blend.

Replacing Heavy Cream

Thickening soups, sauces, gravies

One of the most annoying things about "normal" recipes is how much heavy cream goes into EVERYTHING. I don't use cream or half and half in ANY of my recipes. How do I thicken sauces and soups? I use cornstarch, heated with almond, nonfat, or low carb milk. You can also try, powdered milk, silken tofu, potato flakes, xanthum gum, tempered Greek yogurt... heck, you can even use canned pumpkin puree or blended white beans to act as a thickener agent.

Fat Free & Reduced Fat Cheeses

The Hard To Find Ingredient

It's obvious that you should swap full fat cheese for reduced fat cheese, however, there's another variety that you can try, if you can find it. Fat Free cheese. You can have up to 3 cups of fat free Kraft mozzarella cheese for only 4 points, while 3 cups of regular mozzarella cheese is 41 points! Unfortunately, fat free cheeses are pretty hard to find in most areas. I sometimes find it at Walmart.

Flavored Popcorn Seasonings

They Ain't Just For Popcorn!!

Want a wide range of low calorie, low point, non traditional flavor seasonings that pack a TON of punch? Go the the popcorn aisle at the store and take a look at all the flavors of popcorn sprinkles. Scan them to see the points, but you can use them to flavor desserts, sauces, appetizers... there is a TON of different flavors and brands. My cheese sauce, later in the book, calls for Molly Mcbutter brand cheese powder. You can use one of these though. Every store has them.

Fat Free "Cream Cheese"

Seriously... it's simple

By using cheese cloth, or paper coffee strainers, to strain Greek yogurt overnight, it takes on the texture of softened cream cheese. On the new plan, as long as you don't select 'Diabetic', it's 0 points for you. I often use it in my spreads, dressings, dips even in my frostings for cakes and cupcakes. An alternative if you don't like Greek yogurt, is to run fat free cottage cheese through a food processor, till smooth, THEN strain it overnight.

Flavored Cooking Sprays Instead of Oil

Obvious, but deserves a shout-out

I personally use a TON of butter flavored cooking spray. When seasoning raw meats, I hit both sides with butter flavored or olive oil flavored cooking spray to help flavor the meat. You can also use the butter spray on popcorn. Use the olive oil spray to lightly hit the top of homemade low point hummus or other dishes instead of drizzling olive oil on them. There are tons of ways to use flavored sprays as a seasoning.

Powdered Peanut Butter

Dehydrated and nearly Fat Free PB

Powdered peanut butter, regardless of the brand, is freaking awesome. You can mix it with water to rehydrate it for use as regular peanut butter or you can add the powder to recipes and baked goods to give a PB flavor without all the added mass, points, or stickiness. It's great in everything from smoothies to satay sauces, baking mixes or mixed with pudding or yogurt. The best part being that it's a fraction of the points of regular peanut butter. Allergic to peanuts? There's powdered Almond butter.

Dairy Free Yogurt Hack

Go Go Gadget, TOFU!

When I first started posting recipes for Greek yogurt based salad dressings, then began using strained Greek yogurt instead of Fat Free cream cheese in my frostings... people started asking about something I'd never thought of before. What to use instead of Greek, when you're allergic to dairy?

Greek yogurt is such a huge building block of so many things in system. 2 Ingredient dough, breakfast parfaits, using it in place of sour cream... heck, I even use it to replace Lard in my Tamales. It made me start looking around for an easy alternative. I found one, it works, but it's a bit unconventional. Tofu. Yup... that's right. It's readily available at grocery stores, inexpensive, and doesn't have a strong flavor (unlike Greek). It comes in different levels of firmness. Firm, which you can dent a Buick with. Semi or Medium Firm, which is like a cooled block of cream cheese, then Silken (or soft), which is almost like Plain yogurt.

I blend a 16 ounce block of semi firm tofu with 1/2 cup water, to make a viable replacement for Greek yogurt. It works for 2 ingredient dough and salad dressings. It does "tighten" up a bit in the fridge though, so add more water if necessary. If you want that tang that Greek has, add a splash of lemon juice. After you blend it, you can also strain it again, like my Fat Free "cream cheese", to use it in frostings. Does it taste the same as Greek? No, but it's a great alternative, if you have allergies. It works.

Coating Meat with Flour for 0 Points

ULTIMATE HACK!

This one is a Godsend for if you're planning to 'bread' some meat for baking or frying. The typical way to coat raw meat with flour is to use a TON of it. However, you CAN coat a lot of meat with only 1-1/2 tsp of flour, which is 0 points. Spread all your meat out, then place 1-1/2 tsp of flour into a fine wire mesh strainer/sieve. You know how on cooking shows, they fill them with powdered sugar and lightly tap them over desserts to 'dust' them? Well, you can do the same thing, but using flour. Gently tap the strainer while holding it over the meat, then flip it and dust the other side. You can thuroughly coat 4 thick chicken breasts for 0 points.

DIY Low Point Brown Sugar Substitute

A Little Molasses Goes a Long Way

First off.... YES... I know that you can buy 0 point brown sugar substitutes. Popular ones are Lakanto brand "golden" monkfruit, Swerve, Sukrin Gold, even Truvia has a 0 calorie brown sugar replacement. However... some people don't have access to them, locally. Luckily there's an easy fix. Real brown sugar is simply regular sugar mixed with a little molasses. Well, if you have molasses and any type of sweetener, you can sub it in recipes. 1/4 tsp of molasses is 0 points. If I'm making a dish that calls for 1/4 cup or less of brown sugar, I'll use that much sweetener, then add the 1/4 tsp molasses to the dish.

Substitutions For Food Allergies

Just a few to consider

I'm going to be mentioning a bunch of stuff in here, so let's quit with the bantering.

Allergic to peanuts but need a little peanut butter in a recipe? Puree some garbanzo beans. The flavor's a little different, but it'll work. If you can have sesame seeds, add up to 1/4 tsp sesame oil to the puree.

Allergic to eggs? replace 1 egg in a baked good with 1/4 cup of pumpkin puree or mashed banana. Add a little baking powder if you want to help add a little lift. Bob's Red Mill makes certified Gluten Free All Purpose Flour that already has xanthum gum and other binders in it to help fortify the flour. If you are making a Greek Yogurt based creamy dressing and are allergic to dairy, blend tofu with water. If you want to make one of my cake recipes, that are based on Pillsbury Sugar Free cake mixes, but you're allergic to gluten or splenda, "Swerve" makes a gluten free, sugar free cake mix, that is sweetened with erythritol. Also, "Namaste" brand baking mixes has a ton of ALL allergen free mixes, though they are a little higher in points (not sugar free).

Low Point Pasta Options

Pasta, Pasta!

Want a big bowl of pasta but the thought of the points involved makes your cringe? Well, luckily theres' a few ways around that. First, I'll bring up the obvious, make it yourself. On pages 40-43 of this book, I have detailed instructions showing you how to make your own low point fresh pasta.

If you're more of a visual learner, I have videos showing how to do it, so you can watch me go through the process. If you go head to Youtube, do a search for the following vids:

- *The Guilt Free Gourmet, How to make fresh pasta*
- *The Guilt Free Gourmet, Fresh pasta with a food processor*
- *The Guilt Free Gourmet, Fresh pasta without a pasta machine*

Lastly, if you go into *Connect*, in the app, watch my 2 videos at: *#DHallakLowPointLasagna*. If you watch both videos, I show you how to make a 4 layer, 13x9 lasagna, using only 9 points of pasta.

Aside from that, we still have a couple of options. One is shiritake noodles, commonly called 'magic pasta'. You can find them in the grocery store, next to the tofu, in the refrigerated aisle. Know that they DO NOT HAVE the same texture as traditional noodles. Do not use them for spaghetti or Italian dishes. They work best if used for Asian dishes, due to their slightly firm, springy texture. If yougive them a try, you HAVE TO thuroughly rinse them off first, then boil them for a few minutes. The water solution they come packed in has a similar smell to imitation crab. Hence, whey it's so important to rinse, rinse, and rinse them off first.

For lower point store bought pasta, you can also find lower carb pastas, like 'Caba-nada', in a lot of major grocery stores. They are lower carb egg-noodles. Though you can find similar brands that offer lower carb linguinie, fettucini, etc.

Stretch The Servings with Low Point Fillers

Recipe Building 101

Your recipe has a certain amount of points in it. If that recipe makes 2 servings, it'll be twice the points if it made 4 servings. By bulking up a dish with 0 or low point vegetables or proteins (depending on your plan), you can drastically increase the servings and decrease the points. Pictured to the left, is my awesome pasta salad recipe. I use my Ricotta Gnocchi recipe for the pasta, use sliced, grilled chicken breast for the meat, have it loaded with a TON of roasted 0 point vegetables and wilted spinach, then I have it dressed with some of my low point roasted garlic and onion salad dressing. The points from the ricotta gnocchi get stretched out with a BUNCH more servings, by adding the vegetables and chicken. It stretches the 10 points of ricotta gnocchi and 2 points of my dressing to make enough pasta salad for (6) 1 cup servings. So that gives us an entire cup of freakin' GOURMET gnocchi pasta salad, loaded with grilled vegetables, chicken, wilted spinach and creamy dressing... for just 2 points per serving... on the old-school Blue plan.

Low-ish Point and Calorie Milk & Cream Alternatives

Because of calories and points, I don't really use regular milk or cream in ANYTHING. I pretty much use almond milk, soy milk, or CARBMaster brand (from Kroger stores) lactose free milk in everything. They are all extremely low in points and calories, but equally as important, they are all THICKER THAN REGULAR MILK, which makes them ideal for helping to thicken pudding and sauces.

My coconut cupcakes and cake, call for "coconut flavored beverage", rather than canned, Light coconut milk. I use Silk or So Delicious brands, because they are 2 points for an entire cup of thick and light coconut milk. If your local store doesn't have them (they can be found by the almond milk), you can most likely find an almond/coconut milk blend that you can use in its place. If you are allergic to nuts and can't use almond milk in one of my recipes that calls for it, use ANY low point and calorie milk you can find.

Stevia, Truvia, Monkfruit & Erythritol-Based Sweeteners

Whether people agree with me or not about using them... I have absolutely no problem whatsoever with using Sweeteners. "They aren't natural!" There are plenty of natural sweeteners that are NOT white sugar. My personal favorite is Lakanto brand monkfruit. I have to warn you on one though... "Monkfruit In The Raw" brand is mixed with multidextrine, it has the worst artificial aftertaste ever, in my opinion. Putting "in the raw" behind monkfruit on that package,is horribly misleading. Organic Stevia is a 100% natural sweetener, that even the 2 old men from the muppets can't honestly complain about.

My primary reason for using them is calories. First and foremost, I am most concerned with using anything I can to cut calories from my recipes, without cutting flavor or portion sizes. Using sweeteners instead of sugar, if you have no food sensitivities to them, is a no brainer. 1 cup of sugar has nearly 800 calories... you'd be hard pressed to find any recipe for a sweet bread, pie, or cake, that doesn't require 2 cups of it. By contrast, an entire cup of most sweeteners has 0 calories. I didn't get fat by eating sweetener, and I'm not about to give up desserts or eat tiny portions.

*NOTE: If you choose 'diabetic' in the new survey, some of these sweeteners will get points for you. That's because WW is counting the carbs for the sugar alcohols. Even though it's clearly stated on the packaging that those carbs are NON GLYCEMIC, 0 NET CARBS!! *shrugs* You do you.*

Different Types of Thickeners

Though I must admit that in my recipes, I typically only use cornstarch, I wanted to make sure to point out other commonly available ingredients that you can also experiment with.

- **Cornstarch:** A little bit goes a long way. You can go up to 1-1/2 tsp of cornstarch for 0 points, and up to around 1 Tbsp for only 1 point. Dissolve it in a tiny bit of liquid, then heat it up in a sauce or soup and let it simmer for a few minutes. It will thicken the sauce and you won't need as much of it as you would flour. The typical ratio that I like to use, is 1-1/2 tsp of cornstarch for each 3/4 cup liquid to thicken. Cornstarch is also Gluten Free.
- **Xanthum Gum:** Thickens just as well as cornstarch, but it doesn't need to be heated. You can use it to thicken cold liquids, like salad dressings.
- Gelatine: Great for jellies, gravies, and clear glazes.
- **Potato Starch:** Works just as well as cornstarch, but some folks like it better.
- **Guar Gum:** I don't have much experience with it, but it's readily available at stores.

Tenderizing Meat With Baking Soda

This is the one that I get asked about, more than anything else. "Why in the heck do you put baking soda on your chicken, Daniel!?!?" Well, because of science!!

Baking Soda actually DOES tenderize meat a whoooooole heck of a lot more than you'd think. I'm not talking about dusting meat with a pound of baking soda... that'd taste horrible. However, by making a solution of a little baking soda with a little water, then rubbing it all over your meat and letting it sit for 20-30 minutes, the baking soda actually begins to BREAK DOWN the outer protein walls of your meat. This results in EXTREMELY tender beef, chicken and pork. For 1 to 2 lbs of meat, I dissolve 1/4 tsp baking soda with 2 tsp water. Stir the 2 together, then rub over the meat and let it rest. Trust me.

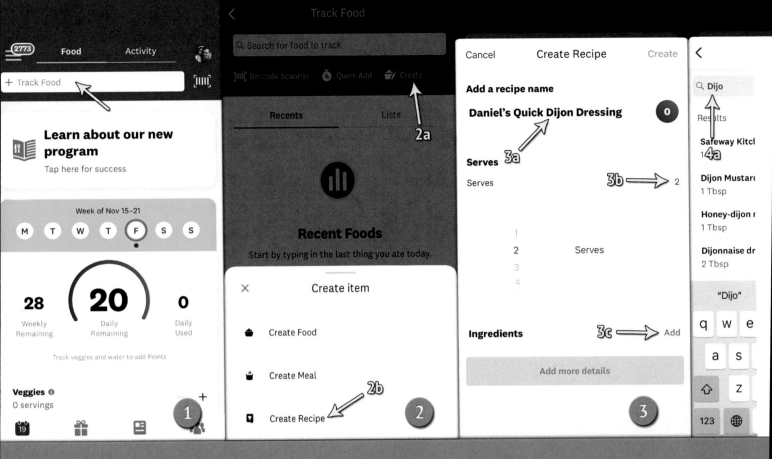

MASTERING

One of the first rewards I set for myself, was if and when I'd lose my first 20lbs, that I could have my mom's old chicken divan casserole Only one problem, I didn't have the recipe. So I went onto the food network's website and found the recipe from a very famous Southern Chef that loves her some butter, ya'll. I decided that I would use that for my Chicken Divan.

I opened up the App's Recipe Builder, entered in the recipe exactly as is, and couldn't believe that 1 single serving was 18 points. NO WAY was I going to eat that. I set about trying to make a healthier version and it completely changed everything. I was able to get that casserole down to 2 points per serving from her 18. It was my "Road to Damascus" moment with Weight Watchers.

I am going to do my absolute best in this section to help walk you through a step by step tutorial of how to do what I do with recipes I want to make WW Friendly. I'm going to talk you through how to enter that same chicken divan recipe that I found online, so that we can modify it together and you can learn to create, tweak and save your own recipes..

Although I'm going to be making this recipe in 'my' personal plan... which is a near-identical replica of the old "Blue Plan", you can easily modify and tweak it, so that it would best work as your own specific 'personal plan'.

Recipe Builder 101

Alright folks, like I said, I'm going to do my best to help you get the fullest benefit out of the Recipe Builder. So, class is in session. For the benefit of the newer folks to the program, I'm going to type this out as if you have NEVER opened up the Recipe Builder in the app before.

NOTE: The process for adding recipes is very similar from your desktop computer on the WW website. On your computer click the "create" button to the right of the search bar on your desktop.

STEP 1: When you open the app on your mobile device, you'll be on your "My Day" screen. Click the "+ Track Food" bar at the top.

STEP 2: On the next screen, click "Create" (*2a*), then, click the *"Create Recipe"* (*2b*) text, when the white pop up appears at the bottom of the screen.

STEP 3: Enter a name for the recipe (*3a*), select how many servings it will be (*3b*), then click to 'Add' your first ingredient.

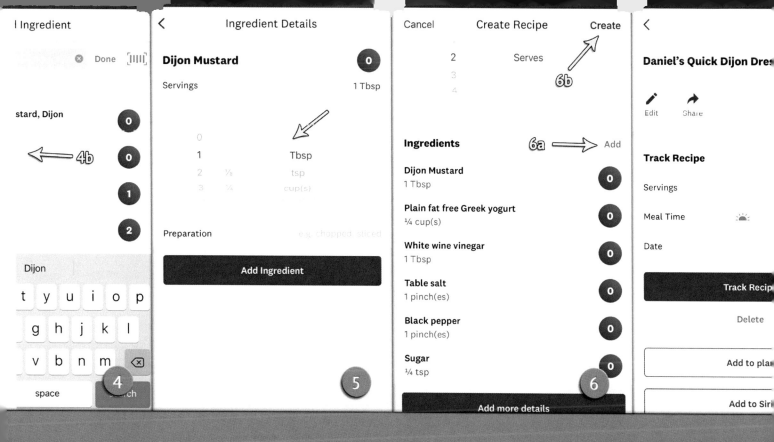

THE RECIPE BUILDER

STEP 4: Alright, now's where the fun begins. *(4a)* This is where you enter in the name to search for ingredients. In this case, I wanted to add Dijon Mustard. As soon as I started typing Dijon, the builder started pulling up possible ingredients underneath. So, I selected 'Dijon Mustard'. *(4b)*. Now, in a lot of cases, the ingredient you might be searching for won't pop up at the top, you'll actually have to scroll down through a list, until you find it. Example: If you search for 'Garlic', actual raw garlic isn't at the top. You'll see listings for garlic chicken, garlic mayonnaise, etc, etc. You'll actually have to scroll down a ways to find a generic listing for 'Garlic'.

STEP 5: Now that I've selected Dijon Mustard, I now have to select how MUCH I want to have in the recipe. For each ingredient you add, you'll be able to select different measurements (tablespoons, teaspoons, cups, ounces, etc). Select the appropriate measurement, then scroll up and down to input the quantity you are using. Example: 1-1/4 tsp, 3 Tbsp, etc. THIS is where you can really tweak the points in your recipes. Play around with it, scroll up and down with different ingredients. Most will gain or lose points at certain amounts. For instance... you can have 1 Tbsp of dijon mustard for 0 points, BUT... once you go over 1 Tbsp it started gaining points. Do you REALLY need 2-1/2 tsp of paprika in a recipe? Or will 2 tsp work just as well... and save you a point? When you're finished choosing your measurement, click 'Add Ingredient'.

STEP 6: Now, repeat the process of adding different ingredients and their measurements *(6a)*, until your recipe is done. When you're finished, click "Create" up at the top right *(6b)*.

WOOOT!!! You just created your first recipe!!!

Recipe Exercise #1: (Full Fat Chicken Divan)

Create a new recipe and name it "AA - TEST RECIPE" so that it's easy to find and delete later. List it as having 8 servings and input the following ingredients and measurements. Do not choose "light sour cream" "reduced fat mayo" etc, use the full fat regular versions of everything. This exercise is to prove a point.

- 20oz Broccoli, cooked
- 6 cups shredded chicken, cooked
- 2 cans of condensed cream of mushroom soup
- 1 cup mayonnaise
- 1 cup sour cream
- 1 cup shredded cheddar cheese
- 1 tablespoon lemon juice
- 1 teaspoon curry powder
- 1/2 cup white wine
- 3/4 cup grated Parmesan
- 1/2 cup plain breadcrumbs
- 3 tablespoons butter

Recipe Builder

Let the Swapping Begin

For purposes of this tutorial, to make it as simple as possible, I am not going to be using things like the fat free cheese hack. We are going to use regular reduced fat cheese and other items that you can easily purchase from the store. So... let's dig in.

Pictured to the right is the in-app point values for the original full-fat Southern recipe. Your mission, should you choose to accept it, is to swap out and substitute these high point/fat/calorie ingredients, for lower point items that would work just as well.

STEP 1: First thing first. I decided that for me personally that I wanted the chicken, cheese and broccoli casserole to be extra cheesy. To further that goal and also to drop the points, I replaced the 2 cans of condensed cream of mushroom soup, with 1 can of "healthy request" condensed cheddar cheese soup. Why the can marked "healthy request?" It has 2 less points than the regular campbell's soup. That saved 9 points. Next, was the big fat-bomb, 1 cup of mayonnaise and 1 cup of sour cream. I replaced them with 2 cup of greek yogurt and 1/2 cup water. I made up for the lost 1/2 cup of bulk, by adding some onion. So, another bucket full of points gone. But... how are we going to thicken it without all the full fat mayo? Cornstarch..... Boom!

STEP 2: Let's get cheesy!!!!
The regular recipe calls for 1 cup of regular shredded cheddar cheese, and 3/4 cups of grated Parmesan cheese. We are going to get rid of that 32 points of combined full fat cheese. I want it cheesier, and meltier, so I replaced the grated parmesan with low fat mozzarella, which saved 4 points. Then swapped the full fat cheddar for reduced fat, saving another 6 points. The creaminess of the mozzarella, vs the original parmesan, will also help offset the lack of regular fatty creaminess from the mayo and sour cream. You can see how all of these subs are quickly making this casserole MUCH healthier, MUCH lower in points and MUCH lower in total fat and calories. But wait, we're not done yet, mis amigos!

STEP 3: Now we're coming into the home stretch, we're at the liquids. So we'll need water for the condensed soup, that's the water we mentioned earlier. Next is the lemon juice, which isn't a problem, then the white wine. Now, we just want the flavor of white wine in the dish. It can be subtle, it doesn't need to kick us in the face. So do you want a slight flavor?.. Try adding just 1 tablespoon of it in with water, want a little more? Add some white wine vinegar. The recipe asks for a 1/2 cup of white wine... we just cut another 3 points.

Original Recipe

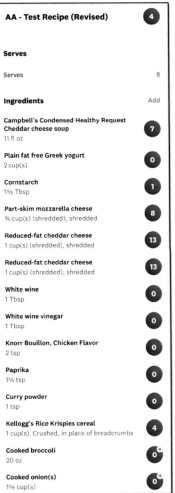

Revised Low Point Recipe

STEP 4: Now, because we have all of this liquid, we don't want our casserole to be runny, but we don't want to thicken it with a buttload of mayo, so what do we do? Cornstarch.... boom. Dissolve it with a tiny bit of water, then stir it in with the canned cheese soup, white wine and other liquids.

We're also going to be eliminating the butter, that's only used to mix with a ton of breadcrumbs, to sprinkle on top of the casserole. Instead, I'm going to crush up 1 cup of rice krispies and use those as the crumbs, it's lower points. Then, we'll put those in a bowl, spray them down with a 0 point amount of butter flavored cooking spray, toss it together, then use that as the topping.... End scene. *applause from the audience*

You just used that coconut on top of your head, to do some creative ingredient swaps, letting you drop Paula Dean's Casserole o' Fat, down 15 points per serving.

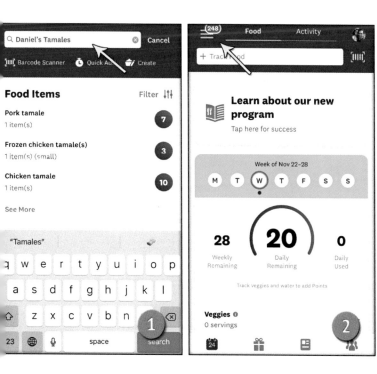

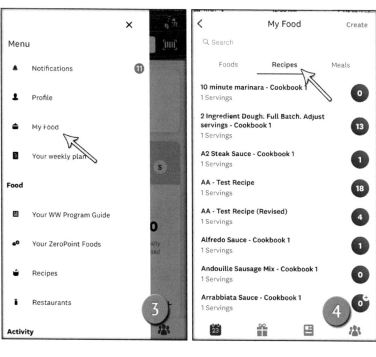

Where Are Your Saved Recipes?

Aye Carumba! Donde Estas Mis Recipes?!?!?!

So you've gone through ALL the hard work of typing out and saving a Gajillion recipes into your own personal App's database. Huzzah! Good for you! But then, the unthinkable happens and you can't find them. Don't worry, it happens. A lot of times you'll click the "+ Track Food" bar up at the top of the screen, ,type in the recipe you're looking for (Daniel's Tamales, for this example)... and they don't pop up. In fact, a lot of times tons of other similar items will pop up, but not your carefully saved recipes. Well, there's an easy way to get to ALL of your saved recipes, so you can search through them alone.

STEP 1:
- You've typed the name of the food you want to find and it doesn't pop up. Don't stress... move to step 2.

STEP 2:
- From the main 'my day' screen of the App, click the 3 horizontal menu bars, up in the top left corner of the screen.

STEP 3:
- Once you click the menu bars, a big menu 'pop up' will appear. It'll list a bunch of helpful tools within the App:
    * Notifications, Profile, My Food, etc.
- Click the link for "My Food".

STEP 4:
- To find your created/saved recipes, in the 'My Food' area, click 'Recipes'. Then you'll be able to scroll down or search through every single recipe you have eeeeeeeever saved into your builder. If there are ever any random recipes you want to delete, simply swipe left to get rid of them. It's like Tinder.... but without the naughtiness.

FOUNDATIONS

Recipes for miscellaneous food items used as the building blocks for other meals

What are Foundation Recipes, and why do they need a section? To me, any recipe that is used as the base, or, dare I say... Foundation for a dish, needs special mention. For example, all of the recipes in my upcoming cookbooks will contain one or more of the following foundation recipes.

These are the foundational components of those dishes, such as fresh pasta, ground turkey chorizo, bratwurst and italian sausage, pie crust, yeast pizza dough, masa and more. I thought it would be extremely helpful if I gathered all of my different foundation recipes and compile them all into this one single section, for easy reference.

Use these as the base for your own recipes that you make within the recipe builder. Have a recipe that calls for high point graham cracker crust? Use my low point pie crust instead. Want to hack down the points in a Lasagna recipe? Use my fresh pasta along with my fat free cheese hack. These are the components from which greater dishes are built.

"... blessed are the lowly foundational recipes that act as a base for more fancy dishes, for they shall bless thine tastebuds ..."
- The Book of Freestyle 10:24-25

Foundation Recipes

Cream Cheese Substitute ... pg 36

Breading 2.0 ... pg 35

Andouille

Smoky and SPICY sausage, popular in Cajun cooking

Asian

Ground turkey or chicken LOADED with asian flavors

This ground meat mixture is meant to give a flavor similar to regular Andouille pork sausage, while cutting fat and calories. I tried to modify a traditional recipe, to have the flavors work with ground turkey. Though this can be used for cooked 'crumbled' ground meat... you can also form it into link-style shapes, or try to make traditional sausages with it, using natural casings.

Serving Info:

Seasoned Mix
Servings: 8
Serving Size: 2oz

 R D
0-0

- last checked 11/14/22 -
Use your mobile device's 'Camera' App to look at this code for nutritional info.

Ingredients:

- 1 pound extra lean ground turkey
- 1/4 tsp baking soda dissolved into 1 tsp water (TRUST ME!)
- 1/4 tsp ground cumin
- 2 tsp paprika
- 2 tsp smoked paprika
- 3/4 tsp salt
- 1/4 tsp black pepper
- 1/2 tsp cayenne pepper
- 1/4 tsp dried thyme
- 1/4 tsp dried sage (or 'rubbed' sage)
- 1/4 tsp ground allspice
- 2 tsp beef flavored bouillon granules (such as 'Knorr' brand)
- 1/2 tsp dry mustard
- 1 Tbsp red wine
- 1-1/4 tsp liquid smoke, hickory flavor
- 4 medium garlic cloves, minced (or, 1 tsp garlic powder)
- 1/2 cup onion, minced

Directions:

- Combine all ingredients in a mixing bowl, until well combined. Allow to sit for 20 minutes, covered.
- Cook as desired.

This mix is so delicious and flavorful, it could easily pass for ground pork when used for Asian dumplings or burgers. I came up with this mix while trying to make a Vietnamese Banh Mi burger and I couldn't believe the texture and flavor explosion. I actually LOVE making this into meatballs, with my sweet & sour sauce.

Serving Info:

Seasoned Mix
Servings: 8
Serving Size: 2oz

 R D
0-0

- last checked 11/14/22 -
Use your mobile device's 'Camera' App to look at this code for nutritional info.

Ingredients:

- 1 pound extra lean ground turkey
- 1 Tbsp Asian "fish sauce"
  It's Pretty much bottled anchovy water. YUM!
- 1/2 tsp ground black pepper (coarse ground, preferably)
- 1/2 tsp ground ginger
- 3-4 medium garlic cloves, minced
- 1 tsp sesame oil
- 2-1/2 Tbsp soy sauce, reduced sodium
- 1/4 tsp baking soda dissolved in 1/2 tsp water *(TRUST ME!!)*
- 1 tsp lime juice
- 1/4 cup green onion, thinly chopped (not the white part)
- 3/4 tsp sesame seeds, toasted in a hot pan for 2-3 minutes.
- 2 tsp chicken or beef flavored bouillon (granules)

Directions:

- Combine all ingredients in a mixing bowl, until well combined. Allow to sit for 20 minutes, covered.
- Cook as desired.

Bratwurst

Ground Turkey Bratwurst that doesn't suck!?

Guten Morgen, friends! I originally came up with this seasoning blend for my Oktoberfest burger, used later in Cookbook 3. It took multiple attempts to finally get the seasoning right. Even though it isn't pork... it tastes great, has nice texture and cuts hundreds of calories .

Serving Info:
Seasoned Mix
Servings: 8
Serving Size: 2oz

- last checked 11/14/22 -
Use your mobile device's 'Camera' App to look at this code for nutritional info.

Ingredients:
- 1 pound extra lean ground turkey
- 2 tsp beef flavored granules
  (in the soup aisle, or in the mexican food aisle, like the "Knorr" brand)
- 1/2 tsp ground cumin
- 1 tsp onion powder
- 1 tsp garlic powder
- 2 tsp smoked paprika
- 3/4 tsp dried mustard
- 1 tsp dried sage (might be in the spices as rubbed sage)
- 1/2 tsp dried marjoram
- 1/2 tsp black pepper
- 1/4 tsp baking soda dissolved in 1/2 tsp water *(TRUST ME!!)*
- 3/4 tsp nutmeg
- 1/2 tsp salt
- 1 tsp caraway seed, toasted (instructions on pg. 47)
- 2 tsp worcestershire sauce
- 1/2 cup diced onion (*OPTIONAL*, for bulk, if desired)

Directions:
- Combine all ingredients in a mixing bowl, until well combined. Allow to sit for 20 minutes, covered.
- Cook as desired.

Breakfast Sausage

99% Fat Free, Low Calorie Breakfast Sausage

There are a lot of different low point breakfast sausage recipes out there that call for ground turkey.... this is mine. Mine's a little more on the maple-side of things, because I like that kind of sausage. In this recipe, the sugar free pancake syrup is completely optional. You can replace it with some maple extract from the baking aisle, if you can't have artificial sweeteners. Also, I HIGHLY recommend using the cayenne pepper. Even if you only use a tiny little 1/8 tsp of it, it makes a huge difference.

Serving Info:
Seasoned Mix
Servings: 8
Serving Size: 2oz

- last checked 11/14/22 -
Use your mobile device's 'Camera' App to look at this code for nutritional info.

Ingredients:
- 1 lb extra lean ground turkey
- 1/2 tsp salt
- 1/2 tsp fresh ground pepper
- 1 tsp dried sage
- 1 tsp dried thyme
- 1-1/4 tsp fennel seed, toasted in a pan, till fragrant, 2-3 mins.
- 1 tsp onion powder
- 1/2 tsp dried marjoram
- 2 tsp 0 point sweetener of choice**
- 1/4 tsp molasses**
- 2 tsp beef flavored granules (like Knorr brand)
- 1/4 tsp baking soda dissolved in 1/2 tsp water *(TRUST ME!!)*
- 2 tsp smoked paprika
- 1-1/2 Tbsp sugar free pancake syrup
- 1/8-1/4 tsp cayenne pepper to taste
- 1/4 tsp liquid smoke, hickory (OPTIONAL)

Directions:
- Combine all ingredients in a mixing bowl, until well combined. Allow to sit for 20 minutes, covered.
- Cook as desired.

Note:
- Feel free to replace the 0 point sweetener and molasses with 2 tsp of 0 point brown sugar substitute.

Chorizo

Low calorie, virtually fat free, delicious Chorizo

Traditional Chorizo is a heavily seasoned, extremely fatty and greasy mixture of ground pork that's loaded with "Pimenton", a type of smoked paprika. If you go to a mexican restaurant and order Chorizo, you'll usually need a good pair of wading pants to get through all of the grease on your plate. My version is really good, has a lot of the traditional flavor, but cuts out 99% of the fat, while still retaining moisture. Mine is ultra low in points, so feel free to add more smoked paprika if you want, but adjust your points accordingly, as always.

Serving Info:

Seasoned Mix
Servings: 8
Serving Size: 2oz

R D
0-0

- last checked 11/14/22 -
Use your mobile device's 'Camera' App to look at this code for nutritional info.

Ingredients:

- 1 lb extra lean ground turkey
- 3 tsp minced garlic (3 med. cloves)
- 2-1/2 tsp chili powder, to taste (normal 'chili powder')
- 1/8 to 1/4 tsp cayenne pepper or chipotle chili powder, to taste.
- 2 canned chipotle pepper in adobo sauce, chopped
- 2 tsp paprika
- 2 tsp smoked paprika
- 1/2 tsp salt
- 1/2 tsp pepper
- 1 tsp dried oregano
- 3/4 tsp ground cumin
- 3/4 tsp ground coriander
- 1/4 tsp ground cinnamon
- 1 tsp cocoa powder (just roll with it)
- 1/4 tsp baking soda dissolved in 1/2 tsp water *(TRUST ME!!)*
- 2 tsp beef flavored granules (like Knorr brand)
- 3 Tbsp apple cider vinegar

Directions:

- Combine all ingredients in a mixing bowl, until well combined. Allow to sit for 20 minutes, covered.
- Cook as desired.

Cuban Picadillo

Delicious latin flavors with lime and cinnamon

This is tied with Kafta for the most flavorful of all of these mixes. It tastes so insanely good. It has strong notes of typical latin flavors, like cumin and oregano... but then you get slapped with little pops of olive, lime and even the exotic hint of cinnamon. It sounds so weird, but it tastes SO GOOD!

Serving Info:

Seasoned Mix
Servings: 8
Serving Size: 2oz

R D
0-0

- last checked 11/14/22 -
Use your mobile device's 'Camera' App to look at this code for nutritional info.

Ingredients:

- 1lb extra lean ground turkey
- 2 tsp beef flavored granules (bouillon)
- 1/2 tsp onion powder
- 1/2 tsp garlic powder
- 2 tsp worcestershire sauce
- 1-1/2 tsp ground cumin
- 1/2 tsp dried oregano
- 1/4 tsp baking soda dissolved in 1/2 tsp water *(TRUST ME!!)*
- 1/2 tsp salt
- 1/4 tsp pepper
- 6 green olives, stuffed with pimientos, drained & chopped (don't get the HUGE olives, you want 8 for 1 point)
- 1 small red bell pepper, finely diced (around 1/2 cup)
- 1 small green bell pepper, finely diced (around 1/2 cup)
- 1 Tbsp raisins, chopped
- 2 tsp 0 point sugar replacement o' choice (I used stevia)
- 2 medium garlic cloves, minced
- 1/4 tsp ground cinnamon
- 1 Tbsp lime juice
- 1/4 cup fresh chopped cilantro

Directions:

- Mix everything together in a large mixing bowl, until well combined. Allow to sit for 20 minutes, covered. Cook until browned.

Greek (Loukaniko)

My version of Greek 'Loukaniko' sausage

Greek Loukaniko is a traditional rustic sausage, seasoned with fennel, oregano, orange zest and cooked, chopped leeks. I took a few liberties with my recipe. A lot of folks voiced not being able to get leeks, so I replaced them with chopped artichokes and spinach in my recipe.

Serving Info:

Seasoned Mix
Servings: 8
Serving Size: 2oz

R D
0-0

- last checked 11/14/22 -
Use your mobile device's 'Camera' App to look at this code for nutritional info.

Ingredients:

- 1lb extra lean ground turkey
- 1/2 tsp ground cumin
- 1-1/2 tsp 0 point sugar replacement o' choice
- 1 tsp ground coriander
- 1/4 tsp black pepper
- 1 tsp dried oregano
- 1/2 tsp dried thyme
- 1 tsp lemon zest OR orange zest, finely minced ***
- 2 tsp beef flavored granules (bouillon)
- 1/2 tsp salt
- 1/2 tsp onion powder
- 1/4 cup canned artichoke hearts, rinsed, chopped (optional)
- 1/2 cup fresh spinach, measured, then chopped
- 2 tsp fennel seeds, toasted in a hot pan for 2-3 minutes
- 3 Tbsp red wine
- 1/4 tsp baking soda, dissolved into 1/2 tsp water

Directions:

- Combine all ingredients in a mixing bowl, until well combined. Allow to rest for a minimum of 20 minutes.
- Cook as desired.

NOTE:
- If you don't have lemon or orange zest, you can use 2 tsp of either lemon or orange juice.

Italian Sausage

Awesome, turkey Italian sausage substitute

When I was trying to lose my weight, when I dove into WW, one thing that I REALLY wanted was Italian sausage. But, let's face it... I'm the Ebenezer Scrooge of Points, so I couldn't make myself use my points on pork sausage. I tried tons of different versions of this recipe, before finally coming up with this baby.

Serving Info:

Seasoned Mix
Servings: 8
Serving Size: 2oz

R D
0-0

- last checked 11/14/22 -
Use your mobile device's 'Camera' App to look at this code for nutritional info.

Ingredients:

- 1 lb extra lean ground turkey
- 1-1/2 tsp fennel seeds, toasted (instructions on pg. 47)
- 1 tsp garlic powder
- 1 tsp onion powder
- 1 tsp dried italian seasoning
- 1/2 tsp dried basil
- 1 Tbsp dried parsley
- 1/4 tsp baking soda dissolved in 1/2 tsp water **(TRUST ME!!)**
- 1/2 tsp salt
- 1/4 tsp fresh ground pepper
- 2 tsp paprika
- 2 Tbsp red wine vinegar
- 2 tsp beef or chicken granules (bouillon)
- red pepper flakes to taste (OPTIONAL)

Directions:

- Combine all ingredients in a mixing bowl, until well combined. Allow to sit for 20 minutes, covered.
- Cook as desired.

Jerk Seasoning

A spicy and savory Caribbean spice blend

No, you don't need to be a meanie-head to make this. "Jerk" is a traditional Jamaican seasoning, normally used on chicken. It typically calls for chopped scotch bonnet peppers, which are hotter than satan's kidney stones. I decided to tone it down a little, by using Habanero peppers, which are easier to find in grocery stores. This mix has it all. Exotic spices, a good deal of heat, a little sweet, and a little acidity from lime juice and zest.

Serving Info:

Seasoned Mix
Servings: 8
Serving Size: 2oz

R D
0-0

- last checked 11/14/22 -
Use your mobile device's 'Camera' App to look at this code for nutritional info.

Ingredients:

- 1lb extra lean ground turkey
- 1/4 green onion, thinly sliced
- 2 medium cloves garlic, minced
- 2 tsp lime juice
- 1 tsp lime zest, minced
- 1-1/2 tsp fresh ginger, finely chopped
- 1 Tbsp soy sauce, reduced sodium
- 1/4 tsp baking soda dissolved in 1/2 tsp water **(TRUST ME!!)**
- 1 tsp fresh thyme, finely chopped
- 2 tsp 0 point brown sugar substitute, OR, 2 tsp regular sweetener and 1/4 tsp molasses.
- 1/2 tsp ground allspice
- 1/4 tsp ground cinnamon
- 1/4 tsp black pepper
- 1/4 tsp nutmeg
- 1/4 to 1/2 tsp cayenne pepper, to taste
- 2 habanero peppers, deseeded, finely diced **(use gloves!!)**
- 2 tsp chicken or beef flavored bouillon

Directions:

- Combine all ingredients in a mixing bowl, until well combined. Allow to rest for a minimum of 20 minutes.
- Cook as desired.

Kielbasa

A smoky, savory and slightly spicy sausage mix

My ground turkey version of Kielbasa, or Polish sausage, has all of the traditional spices of regular beef/pork Kielbasa, as well as my preferred spices to make ground turkey "beefier". We're also going to make up for turkey's lack of fattiness, by adding a little fat free Greek into the mix as well.

Serving Info:

Seasoned Mix
Servings: 8
Serving Size: 2oz

R D
0-0

- last checked 11/14/22 -
Use your mobile device's 'Camera' App to look at this code for nutritional info.

Ingredients:

- 1lb extra lean ground turkey
- 3/4 tsp salt
- 1/2 tsp pepper
- 1-1/2 tsp dried sage
- 1/2 tsp ground ginger
- 2 tsp dried parsley flakes
- 1/2 tsp garlic powder
- 2 tsp paprika
- 2 tsp smoked paprika
- 1/2 tsp ground cumin
- 2 tsp beef flavored bouillon (like Knorr brand)
- 1/2 tsp dried marjoram
- 1 tsp onion powder
- 1/8 tsp ground allspice
- 1/8 tsp ground nutmeg
- 1-1/2 Tbsp fat free plain Greek yogurt
- 1 tsp 0 point sweetener o' choice
- 1/8 to 1/4 tsp cayenne pepper **(TO TASTE)**
- 1 tsp coriander seeds, toasted in a hot pan till fragrant.
- 1/4 tsp baking soda dissolved in 1/2 tsp water **(TRUST ME!!)**
- 1/4 tsp liquid smoke (I used Hickory flavored)

Directions:

- Combine all ingredients in a mixing bowl, until well combined. Allow to rest for a minimum of 20 minutes.
- Cook as desired.

Lebanese Kafta

This baby's like taking a trip to a Kabob House

Kafta is a Lebanese ground meat mixture, usually ground beef or lamb, mixed with a ton of fresh parsley, onion, and seasonings. This is a hybrid of my father's traditional recipe and my own "savory ground turkey". It has a deep, savory, beefy flavor and you won't believe that this is ground turkey.

Serving Info:

Seasoned Mix
Servings: 8
Serving Size: 3oz

R D
0-0

- last checked 11/14/22 -
Use your mobile device's 'Camera' App to look at this code for nutritional info.

Ingredients:

- 1lb extra lean ground turkey
- 2 tsp beef flavored bouillon
- 1 tsp onion powder
- 1 tsp garlic powder
- 1 tsp smoked paprika
- 1/2 tsp ground cumin
- 2 tsp worcestershire sauce
- 1/2 tsp salt
- 1/4 tsp black pepper
- 3/4 tsp ground allspice
- 3/4 tsp ground cinnamon
- 1/4 tsp baking soda dissolved in 1/2 tsp water *(TRUST ME!!)*
- 1/2 cup fresh parsley, finely chopped, loosely packed
- 3/4 cup onion, finely diced/chopped
- 3-4 garlic medium cloves garlic, minced

Directions:

- Combine all ingredients in a mixing bowl, until well combined. Allow to rest for a minimum of 20 minutes.
- Cook as desired.

Savory Mix

A versatile mix that gives a deep, beefy flavor

I use this recipe whenever I need a standard, beefy flavor for a dish. What's the one complaint that you hear about ground turkey from EVERYONE? "It tastes bland...It's dry... It has no flavor". Well, of course it doesn't, so OPEN YOUR SPICE CABINET AND FIX THAT! A lot of thought went into this mix. Think that ground turkey has no flavor? Add beef bouillon, smoked paprika, worcestershire and a touch of cumin. Now you have ground turkey that's saturated with beefy, smoky, earthy flavors.

Serving Info:

Seasoned Mix
Servings: 8
Serving Size: 2oz

R D
0-0

- last checked 11/14/22 -
Use your mobile device's 'Camera' App to look at this code for nutritional info.

Ingredients:

- 1lb extra lean ground turkey
- 2 tsp beef flavored granules
- 1 tsp onion powder
- 1 tsp garlic powder
- 1 tsp smoked paprika
- 1/2 tsp ground cumin
- 1/4 tsp baking soda dissolved in 1/2 tsp water *(TRUST ME!!)*
- 2 tsp low sodium soy sauce
- 2 tsp worcestershire sauce
- 1/4 tsp black pepper
- 1/2 tsp salt

Directions:

- Combine all ingredients in a mixing bowl, until well combined. Allow to rest for a minimum of 20 minutes.
- Cook as desired.

Note:

- This recipe works great as a stand in for ground beef for most recipes, such as burgers, shepherd's pie, sloppy joes, meatloaf and much more.

Taco Seasoning

A simple, but tasty, mix for taco meat

We all grew up with McCormick's taco seasoning packets. That's fine and all, but sometimes you'd rather make your own, so you can control what you're eating. This is my mix, that I use for 99% fat free ground turkey. The additional liquid in the mix is KEY for such lean ground meat, otherwise it won't break into smaller crumbles.

Serving Info:
Seasoned Mix
Servings: 8
Serving Size: 2oz

R D
0-0

- last checked 11/14/22 -
Use your mobile device's 'Camera' App to look at this code for nutritional info.

Ingredients:
- 1 lb extra lean ground turkey
- 1/4 tsp baking soda dissolved in 1/2 tsp water *(TRUST ME!!)*
- 2 tsp beef or chicken granules (bouillon)
- 2 tsp paprika
- 3/4 tsp ground cumin
- 3/4 tsp onion powder
- 3/4 tsp garlic powder
- 2 tsp chili powder
- 1 tsp dried oregano
- 3/4 tsp salt
- 1 tsp unsweetened cocoa powder (just roll with it)
- 3/4 cup water or fat free beef broth, mixed into the meat
--- Then... finish with ---
- 1/2 cup water or fat free beef broth MIXED with
- 1-1/2 tsp cornstarch, dissolved into the liquid

Directions:
- Combine all <u>but the last 2 ingredients</u> in a bowl, mix well. The mixture will be very wet and tacky. Rinse your hands a few times while mixing it to make handling the meat easier. Set aside for 20 minutes.
- Cook the meat in a large pan. While it's cooking, use a spoon to break the meat apart into small pieces.
- When the meat is done, crank the heat up to high, then add the final 1/2 cup liquid, mixed with the cornstarch. Cook at a boil for 1-2 minutes, or until the sauce thickens.

Texas Hot Link

A spicy recipe for nearly fat free hot links

This spicy and smoky mix does a great job of getting the base flavor profile of traditional Texas Hot Links, while still presenting them as low fat and healthy as possible. Flavored with cayenne, 2 kinds of black pepper and diced jalapenos, these are really fantastic. In truth, the base recipe is slightly mild, so you can definitely add more spice, for your palette.

Serving Info:
Seasoned Mix
Servings: 8
Serving Size: 2oz

R D
0-0

- last checked 11/14/22 -
Use your mobile device's 'Camera' App to look at this code for nutritional info.

Ingredients:
- 1 lb extra lean ground turkey
- 1 medium jalapeno pepper, seeds removed, finely chopped
- 4 Tbsp onion, finely minced/chopped
- 1 to 1-1/2 tsp cayenne pepper, to taste (I used 1)
- 1 tsp black peppercorns. Place into a ziplock bag then crush
- them with a mallet, creating coarse bits/chunks
- 1 tsp cracked (coarse ground) black pepper
- 2 medium garlic cloves, crushed and finely minced
- 2 tsp paprika
- 2 tsp smoked paprika
- 1 tsp garlic powder
- 1 tsp unsweetened cocoa powder
- 3/4 tsp salt
- 2 tsp dried sage *(may also be called 'rubbed sage' at your store)*
- 1/2 tsp ground cumin
- 2 tsp worcestershire sauce
- 2 tsp beef flavored garnules/bouillon
- 3 Tbsp fat free beef broth
- 1/4 tsp baking soda, dissolved into the beef broth

Directions:
- Mix everything together in a large mixing bowl, until well combined. Let rest 20-30 minutes. Cook as desired.

NOTES:
- This is mildly spicy. Feel free to add more heat, if you want.

Things You'll Need:

Chicken & Beef Flavored Granules

Add Instant Deep Flavor

Wish that ground turkey tasted more like beef or chicken? IT CAN! There are many different brands of bouillon at your local grocery store, but they are not all created equal. Some are lower or higher in points, sodium and calories than others. Most Walmarts carry the Knorr brand, which I use in anything that has ground turkey. While most brands will turn to 1 point at 2 or 3 teaspoons, Knorr stays at 0 points until you use 3-1/2 teaspoons. At the majority of supermarkets, you most likely won't find it in the soup aisle, which is where you'd THINK to find it. 99% of the time it'll be in the aisle with the Mexican or Latin foods, even at Walmart. Scan any brand of granulated bouillon that you find, but you want one that'll let you have at least 2 tsp for 0 points. If you can't find one, get what you can, but adjust your points if necessary, per recipe. Leave out granules, if using ground Beef.

Rinse Your Hands! (say whaaaaaa?)

Stop Being So Tacky, Baby!

Ok folks, this is a reeeeally simple way to handle meat mixtures, when they're sticky and tacky... wet your hands. No, I'm not kidding, it's that easy. Most of my meat mixes are pretty sticky when you are mixing all of the seasonings and spices together. The meat clings to your fingers and the sides of the bowl... it's frustrating, . In the past, I'd advocate for using cooking sprays, but this is better. When mixing the meat and it begins to stick to your hands, run a little water onto your hand, then get back to mixing. After 2-3 times, the meat forms into a perfect, non sticky ball. It's easier to mix, it's easier to form into patties or into meatballs... Plus, it adds additional moisture into the meat, which is something that ground turkey lacks anyways.

Mixing this bit of water into the meat, not only makes it easier TO mix... it gets locked into the meat by the baking soda trick that's coming up. Which results in juicier cooked meat.

Meatballs

Make ANY of these mixes into meatballs

With a 1lb batch of the meat mixes, use a 1 Tbsp measuring spoon to scoop & form small cocktail sized meatballs. You can get around 30 out of 1 pound, or 15 2 Tbsp ones. I bake them at 400 degrees. For smaller ones, I bake them for 11-12 minutes and 14-16 minutes for larger ones.

Baking Soda

What'chu talkin 'bout, Willis??

I wish I could explain the science behind it, but this is a legit game changer. I was browsing an old French cooking site one night, and came upon a technique for making ground meat awesome. For every 1lb of ground meat, mix in 1/4 tsp of baking soda dissolved with 1/2 tsp of water, then allow the meat to rest for 20 minutes before cooking. It completely changes the texture of the meat. It retains a TON of it's own moisture. You know how when you normally cook ground turkey, it's swimming in a pool of it's own liquids? Who wants grey meat! Doing this locks in so much liquid, that the meat ends up more juicy AND it browns in the pan soooo much better. It's a flippin' Vatican-worthy miracle, imho. Ground turkey ends up having a texture closer to cooked ground pork, which makes these seasonings REALLY sing. Give it a try, you won't regret it. **NOTE: This trick helps tremendously with making the meat plump up and retain moisture. It's fantastic with 'crumbled' meat, broken up in a pan while cooking. HOWEVER... be advised: Don't cook the meat over a direct open-flame. It can develop a very thin, hard exterior. Avoid HIGH heat.**

Burger Patties

THEY COOK FAST!!!!

This isn't as simple as just mixing the meat, form patties and cooking. 99% fat free ground turkey cooks fast. Too long, and it's dry cardboard. If you like thinner burger patties, mix up a 1lb batch of meat, then section it into 8 portions (pictured). Preheat a pan over medium heat for a minute, till water sizzles on it. Cook the thin patties for 2 minutes per side. If you like thicker 1/4lb patties, section the meat into 4 quarters, form into patties, then cook 3 minutes per side. If you cook these too long, they dry out and the exterior gets very hard, from the baking soda. Cook them right and they'll blow your mind.

Cocoa Powder

PSYCH! That's not ground beef!!!!

Here's a cool trick, if you want to make your ground turkey burgers actually LOOK like ground beef. In any of my meat seasoning recipes, add 2-3 tsp of unsweetened cocoa powder to the mix. But don't add it dry. The trick is to mix the cocoa with a little bit of water, to form a paste, then mix it in with the other seasonings. This will cause the meat to take on a darker hue. That small amount will adds an earthy note, rather than a chocolate flavor. It also complements the cumin in most of the mixes.

2 Ingredient Dough

RECIPE INFO
R D
13-15
Points shown
for entire batch

~ last checked 11/14/22 ~
Use your mobile device's Camera App to
look at this code for nutritional info.

The simple yet versatile dough recipe that keeps us sane

If you've been in-program for any length of time you KNOW how much you missed your bread when you first started. I'm including this in the book because there are a lot of new people who still view 2 ingredient dough as a mystery and ask in Connect "How do you make it? What's in it?" For you new folks, this dough is so incredibly versatile, it truly is the kitchen chameleon. I use this stuff for everything. breakfast pizzas, bagels, steamed for Asian inspired dumplings, thrown it into a hearty low point chicken and dumplings, strombolis, biscuits, impromptu projectiles, the list goes on and on.

Ingredients:

- 1 cup Self Rising flour
- 3/4 cup Fat Free Greek Yogurt
- additional water IF NEEDED

Directions:

1 Combine the Flour and Yogurt in a mixing bowl until well combined and formed into a ball.

2 Remove from bowl and place on cutting board dusted with flour.

3 Basic cooking method:
Bake at 375 for 18-20 min.

Various Applications:

- Quarter the dough as pictured below, and use the 4 separate sections for a variety of uses, such as:
Bagels, Biscuits, flattened into rounds to make 4 small personal sized pizzas, and much more.
- Cut the dough into 1/8th's instead of 1/4's to make small dough balls for use as bread knots, small dessert bread bites and appetizers.
- Roll the dough out into long ropes and slice it into small dumplings for use in low point chicken and dumplings.
- Steam the dough to make asian buns.

- If you roll out the dough ball into 1 large round pizza dough rather than sectioning it into quarters, you can use it to make a regular sized medium pizza or a larger sized thin crust pizza.
- **_WATER:_** If you don't want to use yogurt, you can use water instead. Take your 1 cup of flour, then mix in 1/3 cup water. It'll still be a little too thick, so add 1 additional Tablespoon at a time, mixing till the dough JUST comes together. It should be just a little less than 1/2 cup.
- Another version is "**_3 ingredient dough_**". Use 2 cups self rising flour, 1 cup yogurt and 2 eggs. Mix together and portion just like normal. It's more airy and fluffy.

** *Cook temp & time vary depending on application*

(1) dough ball portion

(4) 1/4 portions

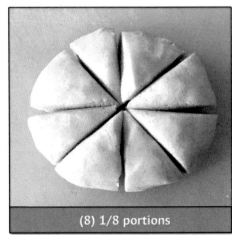

(8) 1/8 portions

Pizza Dough

If you are looking for a fast, reliable and easy way to make a basic pizza crust that's easy to portion for different amounts of Points, then 2 ingredient dough is a godsend. You can use a 1 cup dough ball to flatten/stretch into a good medium sized thin crust pizza that will only cost 16 points all together in crust. For a comparison, the ready-made pizza dough available at major grocery store chain "*Trader Toes*" *cough* is over 35 points.

You can also make 4 personal sized pizzas out of the 1 cup dough ball by cutting it into equal 1/4's, each one being 4 Points. When rolled out they are each the size of a personal sized pizza. Or if you want a Small sized pizza, simply cut the dough ball in 1/2 for 2 small pizzas that are 8 points for each crust. Though cook times vary depending on each person's preference, typically folks bake their 2 ingredient pizzas at 400-425 degrees for between 12-16 minutes, depending on how they like their crust.

Bagels, Biscuits, and Preztels

For those of us that aren't nutcase carb-cutters like some of the trend "diets" turn you in to, using 2 ingredient dough to make bagels, biscuits and pretzels is a game changer in our weight loss journey. For regular sized bagels, biscuits, and pretzels you should quarter the 1 cup dough ball, making (4) 4 point sections. For bagels, roll each section into a thick rope and then twist it into a round bagel shape. Pretzels are prepared in the same way except the rope of dough is twisted into a pretzel shape. You can then spray each piece with butter flavored cooking spray, sprinkled it with your desired seasonings and bake. Typical baking directions for bagels is: 350 degrees for 20 minutes, then turn up the heat to 450 degrees for a final 2-3 minute to brown the top a little more. For REAL, browned and chewy bagels, boil a large pot of water with 1/4 cup of baking soda in it. When your raw dough is shaped into rounds, boil them for 30 seconds on each side. Take the boiled bagels out of the baking soda bath, then bake them at 425 until dark brown, about 13-15 minutes. They are 10x more awesome that way.

Snack Sized Bites

Other than pizzas and big delicious bagel sized fluffy goodness, there are even more ways to utilize this dough. Rather than sectioning it into (4) 1/4 sections, you can section the 1 large dough ball into 8 separate smaller sections. 1 piece is 2 points.

You can use these smaller sections for a ton of different small bites and appetizer ideas such as bite sized pretzel nuggets, rolling the rounds in your sweetener of choice and cinnamon, form the sections into small flat tortilla-like rounds with a filling in the center and then roll them up into a stuffed bread ball with any number of fillings.. the options are endless. Cooking temperatures and bake times vary depending on what type of snack sized appetizer you are trying to make. A quick search online or in Connect will find tons of recipe ideas.

Empanadas/Stuffed Pockets

2 ingredient dough is also a fantastic vehicle to make savory stuffed breads and pastries. Using the same exact principles as all of the other applications, you can simply fold your preferred filling of choice inside two layers of the dough to make sweet or savory stuffed empanadas, calzones, stromboli, baked panini sandwiches, baked breakfast pockets filled with scrambled eggs, cheese, veggies... you are only bound by the limits of your culinary imagination.

You can find hundreds of delicious recipes and ideas on Connect or any number of websites such as pinterest, emilybites and skinnytaste.

Breading 1.0 (revised)

How to Use Low Calorie, Low Carb "Keto" Bread, to Make Low Point Breadcrumbs

I first made my cookbooks, there WAS no widely available Keto bread, now, you can find it in most major supermarkets and Walmarts. Because of it's wide availability now, I decided to revise this cookbook to include it's use. Though a lot of brands are available at 1 point per slice, you'll need to experiment to find the brand(s) you like best.

Ingredients:

- 5 slices of ANY BRAND "Keto", sliced bread. I personally love the *'Signature Select'* brand, which is available at most Albertsons, Vons, Kroger, Ralphs and other Kroger 'family' stores. (Signature Select is 5 slices for 4 points)

Things You'll Need:

- An oven
- Baking sheet pan(s).
- Food processor OR a gallon ziplock bag with a rolling pin
- A 10" or 12" pan.

Serving Info:

Yield: 1-1/4 cups crumbs. Make's enough breading to coat a 1964, Mint Green Buick Skylark

R   D
4-4
Points shown are for the ENTIRE BATCH

- last checked 12/06/22 -
Use your mobile device's 'Camera' App to look at this code for nutritional info.

Directions:

1. Take 5 slices of your preferred "Keto" bread. Slice them into squares and lay the cut pieces onto a foil-lined baking pan. Arrange them in a SINGLE LAYER. Use more than 1 pan if you don't own 1 large pan. Having the bread in a single layer is important.
2. Preheat your oven to 250 degrees. Once it comes up to temperature, bake the bread for 20 minutes, then remove from the oven and let cool for 15 minutes.
3. (2 options). *Option 1:* Place the cooled bread into a food processor, pulse a few times, then process till they are broken down to crumbs. Or.. *Option 2:* Place the bread into a bag and use a rolling pin to crush it all into crumbs.
4. Heat a large pan over medium heat for 1 minute, then add the crumbs. DO NOT MOVE THE PAN!! Let the crumbs sit in place and cook. EVERY 30 SECONDS, stir and toss the crumbs around, then leave them alone for another 30 seconds, then toss again. Repeat till they take on a slightly uniform golden hue, like in the bottom left picture. *(Mine took 7 minutes)*
5. Pour the hot crumbs back onto the foil of the baking pan and spread them out. Let cool to room temperature. Once cooled, store in an air tight container. Done.

NOTES:

1. You can use ANY brand of Keto bread you want. *I used Signature Select, which is 5 slices for 4 points.* If you use a different brand, adjust your recipe's points accordingly.
2. Going forward, I will still be using "breading 2.0" as my default breading in recipes, because not everyone has access to Keto bread. If you use Breading 1.0 instead, adjust your recipe's points.

Toasted Breading 2.0

I wouldn't recommend using Cocoa Krispies, but that's just me.

Snap Crackle Pop, Rice Breadiiiiiiing

If I already show you how to make bread crumbs with Keto bread, why show you how to make crumbs with Rice Krispies?? Simple. Not everybody across the US has access to 1 point per slice Keto bread (that doesn't suck), but everyone has access to Rice Krispies... I'm helpful like that.

Breading:
- 1-1/4 cup crispy rice cereal (like rice krispies). Place it in a ziplock bag and <u>lightly crush it</u>, don't pulverize it.
- 1-1/2 tsp plain breadcrumbs
- 2 tsp panko breadcrumbs
- 1/4 tsp salt
- 1/4 tsp cracked black pepper
- 1/4 tsp garlic powder
- 1/4 tsp onion powder

Egg Wash:
- 2 large eggs
- 1 tsp baking powder
- 1 Tbsp dijon mustard
- 1 Tbsp water

Additional Ingredients/Equipment: (optional, only needed if you're breading meat)
- 1-1/2 tsp all purpose flour
- fine mesh wire strainer/sieve.

Servings Info.:

Yield: about 2/3 cup breading
Servings: Depends on how you use it. It can bread 4 good sized chicken breasts, around 30 chicken chunks, or a whole tray of onion rings.

RECIPE INFO   R D
1-1

- last checked 11/14/22 -
Use your mobile device's 'Camera' App to look at this code for nutritional info.

Bread Up To 30 Pieces

'Dusting' Meat with Flour

Directions:

1. Add all the listed 'breading ingredients' into a large ziplock bag. Lightly crush the breading until it has the same texture as panko breadcrumbs (coarse crumbs, pictured to the right).
2. Heat a pan over medium heat for 1 minute, pour in the coarsely crushed breading. Heat for 5-6 minutes, tossing every 30 seconds, till the dry ingredients take on a uniform and lightly golden hue. Set aside to cool.
3. ***If using to bread a protein***, place the 1-1/2 tsp of flour into a wire mesh strainer. In the same way you'd dust powdered sugar over a dessert, tap the mesh a few inches over the meat, to lightly dust both sides with flour. You can 'flour' 4 chicken breasts in this way for 0 points.
4. When ready to use the breading, prepare the egg wash: Whisk together the 2 eggs, set aside. In a small dish, stir together the baking powder, dijon mustard and water into a smooth, thick paste. Whisk into the beaten eggs. It will slightly thicken the egg wash.
5. Use according to your recipe's directions. Which usually involves coating the protein in flour, dipping it into the egg wash, then coating it with crumbs. Bake as directed by your recipe.

Toasted vs. Untoasted Breading

UNTOASTED

TOASTED

"Cream Cheese" Substitute

Turning Greek Yogurt into a fat free Cream Cheese Substitute

DIY Fat Free "Cream Cheese" Substitute

First off, I need to give credit where it's due and thank "*@mickeydoyle5*" from Connect for tipping me off to this ingredient hack that I had never heard of before. Once I heard about it I HAD to try it considering how much fat free cream cheese I go through with my cupcakes. THIS STUFF IS AWESOME!!! Make sure that you use a Greek Yogurt with a very mild "tang" to it, as a lot of Greek Yogurts have a very sharp taste that sucks the life & happiness out of desserts normally. I used Chobani Fat Free Greek Yogurt, though my ABSOLUTE FAVORITE is FAGE 0%. Fage is a little pricier but it has the least amount of yogurt tang of all the major brands. It is an almost perfect match to a slightly softened cream cheese with juuuust a tiny bit of bite to it. I personally think that it works as a wonderful sub for cream cheese in dips, spreads and in appetizers. Some folks have been using this in cheesecake recipes with success, which inspired me to start using it in place of cream cheese for my frostings.

Yields: 4 cups

Servings: The servings is completely dependent on the application for which you plan to use the strained yogurt. Below, I will post the TOTAL POINTS for the entire container's worth of yogurt. Use as much or as little as your recipe requires.

Serving Info:

Yield: 4 cups
Servings: n/a
Serving Size: n/a

R D
0-7
Points for the
ENTIRE batch

- last checked 11/14/22 -
Use your mobile device's 'Camera' App to
look at this code for nutritional info.

*This is the amount of points for the **ENTIRE** 4 cup yield. Your points per serving will be dependent upon what 0 point foods are allowed on your plan, as well as how you intend to use it.*

0 point creamy awesomeness

What You'll Need:

- 35oz FAGE (or other mild) Fat Free Greek Yogurt
- Cheese Cloth (or paper coffee filters)
- Strainer
- Large Bowl
- Plastic Wrap

Directions:

1 Attach or set a plastic or metal strainer onto a large bowl or pot in such a way that the strainer will not come in contact with any liquid that drips to the bottom.
2 Line the bowl of the strainer with 6-8 layers of cheesecloth or paper coffee liners (much cheaper).
3 Pour all of the Greek Yogurt onto the cheesecloth.
4 Cover it all with plastic wrap and set in the refrigerator for at least 24 hours (mine was fine at 24).
5 Store in an air tight container for up to 1 week and use in place of regular cream cheese.

Note:

- If you are unable to get cheese cloth, you can line your strainer with a few layers of paper coffee filters.

How To Make It Melt

There has always been one constant truth in the Universe, that Fat Free Cheese can't melt. Actually it can, it's just always done a really bad job of melting. (It sucks at it, actually.)

One afternoon while cooking I accidentally dropped some fat free cheese on the kitchen counter and it landed up against a little dab of yogurt. I was feeling lazy and decided to clean it up later. However when I came back, the two had kind of melded together, which gave me the idea to try this.

By mixing ANY amount of fat free shredded cheese with roughly 1/2 as much fat free plain or greek yogurt, then using it as a spread, you can "cheese" a pizza, lasagna, casserole, any dish you want, for virtually no points compared to regular cheese. It sounds so wrong... but it's so right. Once exposed to high heat, the yogurt and cheese both melt together..

Fat Free Cheese Hack

How To Make Fat Free Cheeses Melt Like Regular Cheese

Ingredients:

- Any amount of Fat Free Shredded Cheese
- Roughly 1/2 to 3/4 as much Fat Free Plain or Greek Yogurt

Directions:

1 Take any amount of Fat Free Shredded Cheese *(or low fat cheese if you would like to make that more melty as well)* and mix it in a mixing bowl with the yogurt until well combined into a thick ricotta-like sticky mixture.
2 Spread or dollop the cheese onto the surface of the dish you would like it to melt on. Cook in the same manner that you would regular cheese. (IE: Baked into a casserole, on top of Chicken Parmesan, etc)

COOKING TIPS:

- A huge benefit of this versus just rinsing off the cheese to help it melt is that the yogurt adds volume to the cheese, stretching it further in your recipe. Add 1 cup of yogurt to 2 cups of cheese and you now have a lower point stand-in for 3 cups of cheese.

- The "Point" value for this technique is based entirely upon how much fat free cheese you decide to use, as well as what 0 point foods are allowed on your 'personal' plan. If you get fat free Greek yogurt for 0 points, this lets you 'cheese' an entire pan of lasagna for only 4 or 5 total points.

Points & Servings:

The points and number of servings is completely dependent upon how much of the cheese you use and how you will be using it. You will need to figure out the points for yourself, based upon your needs.

Masa & Tortillas

The Latin American Dough For Tortillas, Tamales, Sopes, & more

Latin American cuisine would be nowhere without Masa, a dough made from very finely ground corn, which is used to make Tortillas, Tamales, Gorditas, Sopes... it is everything in Latin cooking. Think of it like the all purpose flour that you're used to using for biscuits, rolls, pizza dough, and other common baked goods. The flour required to make Masa is in most all grocery stores, typically found in either the Latin/Ethnic section or by where the Cornmeal is sold, sometimes labeled as "Maseca, Instant Tamale Mix." Note, this is NOT a traditional recipe, this is my version. Because I want them to be healthy, I'm using yogurt instead of lard. This makes the masa softer and also helps the texture should you choose to make tamales by adding the additional baking powder.

Ingredients:

- 2 cups Masa Harina, Maseca, or other brand Instant Corn Masa (corn flour NOT cornmeal!!)
- 1-1/4 cup water
- 1/2 cup Fat Free Plain or Greek Yogurt
- 1/2 tsp salt
- Additional water if needed for mixing
  *** (add 2tsp baking powder if being used to make Tamales)
  *** (you can use fat free chicken broth instead of water, to add more flavor to your masa)

SERVING SIZE & POINTS:

- The servings & points vary, depending on how much masa you use, as well as which plan you are on, due to the Greek yogurt. For tortillas I use 1/16 portions, for tamales I use 1/4 portions. **_The points listed below are for 1/16 portions_**, which is actually 1/8 of each of the 2 big masa balls. **(pictured below)**

Yield: 2 big masa balls
Servings: 16
Serving Size: 1/16 portion

- last checked 11/14/22 -
Use your mobile device's 'Camera' App to look at this code for nutritional info.

Directions:

1. In a large mixing bowl, combine the corn flour, 1-1/4 cups water, yogurt, and salt. Mix thoroughly until you form a semi-firm masa ball. If masa appears dry while mixing, add additional water as needed.

2. Remove masa to a cutting board, and cut into 2 equal sized, large masa balls. Then portion each one into 1/4's and then into 1/8's sized portions.

3. Roll each one of the 16 small masa sections into a circular ball. Then, on a flat surface, use your palm and fingers to press the dough balls into tortilla sized rounds.

4. For perfectly uniform tortillas, you can use a traditional tortilla press to form them. They are fairly inexpensive and can be purchased at most ethnic grocery stores, walmarts, or online, for around $10.-15. Get a metal one.

5. To cook the tortillas, heat a skillet, griddle, or large pan, till hot, over on medium-high heat. Cook each tortilla for around 45 seconds to 1 minute per side.

6. Keep tortillas warm by placing them in a covered container, or place them on a plate covered with a dish cloth. Tortillas are best served warm... unlike revenge.

A FEW DIFFERENT USES:

A) Sopes - Traditionally, the base is made from a circle of fried masa with sides pinched up to resemble a shallow cup. However for WW purposes you should spray it with cooking spray and then bake it. This can then be topped with any number of toppings. Bake the shells at 350 degrees for 10-15 minutes.

B) Tamales - If you are a WW member, you can view a video in Connect where I show how to make 3-4 point Tamales. Search for **#dhallaktamales** and scroll down to my DIY Tamale video.

C) Arepas - Arepas are awesome. For best results use a 3 point 1/4 cup section of the Masa dough, form it into a 1/2" thick tortilla round. For the non-fried WW version, cook it on a hot griddle or pan for 45 seconds on each side, and then remove it from the heat and slice it ALMOST completely in half down its length like a big pocket. Stuff it with fillings of your choice, then return it to heat.

D) If you need me to explain what a Taco is... put down this book. Put it down. No really, put it down. No food for you.

COOKING TIPS:

- You can easily HALVE this recipe if you don't want to make a big batch.
- If you plan to make Tamales OR Arepas, make sure to add 1 tsp of baking powder to each cup of flour that you use to help them fluff up a little bit.
- If you would like to NOT use the yogurt in this recipe due to dairy allergies, you can replace it with an equal amount of silken tofu.
- If you would like an even MORE chewy tortilla, you can substitute 1/4 cup of the corn flour with 1/4 cup of all purpose flour. I personally love the texture that way... but I'm a full-on Gringo.
- If you buy a tortilla press, I would recommend a metal one. They are a few dollars more, but they are more durable. I've broken 2 plastic ones from the hinges breaking with too much pressure.
- Instead of a tortilla press you can put one of the balls of masa between 2 layers of plastic wrap and press down with a pot.
- For more savory tortillas add 1/2 tsp garlic and onion powders to the masa.

Two of the biggest heartaches you hear in Connect are how much people miss pastas (not whole wheat!) and how many points they blow on pasta dishes. I used to think the same way. I went MONTHS without having pasta because I didn't want to spend the points. Then I started looking into it and realized that making your own pasta is lower in points, calories, carbs and is tastier than the store bought dried stuff. Plus, you get A LOT more pasta for the points.

Pasta Basics

Make Your Own Low Point, Low Calorie Pasta

Ingredients:

- 2 cups of all purpose flour (or your flour of choice)
- 3 large eggs
- 1/2 tsp salt (optional)
- 2 Tbsp water
- 5 sprays, olive oil cooking spray
- 1/4 tsp olive oil
- additional water for mixing, as needed, 1 tsp at a time
  ** *up to 1 additional Tbsp of flour, for dusting*

Directions:

1. In a large mixing bowl or stand mixer, combine the flour, eggs, salt, olive oil, cooking spray and 2 Tbsp of water to form a dough ball. The mixture will be dry, so add water as needed to help the dough come together. We aren't adding all of the water all at once because we want to cut down on how much flour we have to use for dusting later on. Wet dough = bad.

2. Remove dough to a cutting board, and cut into 2 equal sized dough balls. I typically wrap and keep 1 of them in the freezer so that I can thaw it out and have ready-made pasta dough at a later time. For this recipe, we will assume that you are doing the same.

Serving Info:

Yield: 2 large dough balls
Servings: 8
Serving Size: 1/4 portion

R D
3-3

- last checked 11/15/22 -
Use your mobile device's 'Camera' App to look at this code for the nutritional info.

3. Take 1 of your halved pasta dough balls, and cut it into (4) 1/4 portions, just like when you section 2 ingredient dough. Next, roll each one of the 1/4 sections into 4 small dough balls.

4. The dough balls are each 3-4 points, depending upon your personal plan. Points may vary dependent upon whether or not you can have eggs as a 0 point food. If not, adjust your points accordingly.

5. Use your hand and a rolling pin to flatten one of the 1/4 cup pasta balls into a roughly rectangular flat shape. *(Read Notes for instructions for dusting the dough)***

6. You are trying to shape your flattened dough balls to fit length-wise across most of the pasta makers guide-track.

7. With the pasta-width adjustment at its widest setting, run the pasta through the sheet rollers 3-4 times, then adjust the knob on the machine to make the rollers 1 step closer together.

8. After every 3-4 passes through the rollers, continue to make the pasta sheet thinner and thinner, stopping after the 2nd from the thinnest setting.

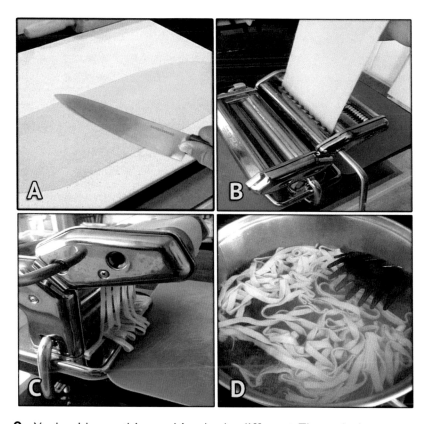

9. Yeah... I know this machine looks different. These 4 pics were taken 7 months apart, with two different pasta makers. 🤷 **(A)** Use a knife to cut your pasta sheet in half, then use a few taps of the remaining flour in your wire strainer, to lightly dust the pasta sheet on both sides. **(B)** Move hand crank to the hole for the linguini cutter. Hold one of the pasta sheet halves over the unit, positioning the bottom of the sheet against the cutting blades. **(C)** Turn the hand crank, while lowering the pasta sheet into the blades. **(D)** As soon as the noodles are cut, drop them into a pot of boiling water. Use a utensil to stir and separate them. Boil for 2 minutes then remove from water and strain. Repeat until all of the pasta is rolled out, cut into noodles and boiled. Use immediately by stirring them into a sauce. If you need to save them for later, rinse the noodles off with cool water and store in a ziplock bag in the fridge. Reheat by putting them back into boiling water for a few seconds.

COOKING TIP:
- ***DUSTING:*** Traditionally, chefs don't "dust" dough with flour, they freakin' DUMP fist fulls of flour onto it. For this recipe, take 1-1/2 tsp of flour and put it into a fine mesh wire strainer. When you need to dust your dough with flour, lightly tap the strainer over the dough instead. Also, you can lightly spritz the dough with cooking spray, as seen in my Youtube video for making low point pasta dough and noodles.
- If you are making lasagna I would highly recommend boiling the pasta sheets first then rinsing them off. Boiling them will make them get MUCH bigger, plus it will give them a slightly firmer texture.
- If you do not have a stand mixer to mix your dough you can either mix it by hand in a mixing bowl, or you can actually mix the dough VERY quickly in a food processor. Check out my video in **Youtube** channel, ***"The Guilt Free Gourmet"*** to find the food processor pasta dough video.
- If you are allergic to gluten, Bob's Red Mill has a great certified Gluten Free, Celiac-friendly, All Purpose Flour, available at most major markets.

Ricotta Gnocchi

Making fresh Ricotta Gnocchi without special equipment

As much as I enjoy making pasta from scratch, most folks in WW don't. Let's face it... it's intimidating. I needed to figure out a way to show people how easy it could be to make their own delicious pasta, without needing any special equipment or pasta machines. Well, now all people have to do is make dough, roll it into ropes, cut it into nuggets and boil. Done.

The KEY to these dumplings is that you want to cut them small. They are not meant to be the bulk of a dish. Fortify them with lots of 0 point veggies, meats, and a low point sauce. You want to stretch the 1 serving of gnocchi as far as you can. They are the star of a dish, not the bulk of it.

Serving Info:

Yield: 2 large dough balls
Servings: 8
Serving Size: 1/4 portion

RECIPE INFO

R D
4-4

- last checked 11/15/22 -
Use your mobile device's 'Camera' App to look at this code for nutritional info.

NOTES:
- You can use fat free cottage cheese instead of ricotta. If you do, I'd add an extra Tablespoon or 2, to make the dough even softer.

Ingredients:

- 2 cups All Purpose Flour *(or your preferred flour)*
- 1 tsp baking powder
- 2 large eggs
- 1/2 cup Low Fat Ricotta Cheese
- 1/2 tsp salt
- 1/4 tsp olive oil
- olive oil cooking spray ***
- additional water to mix (around 1/4 cup)

Directions:

1. In a large mixing bowl, combine the flour, baking powder, eggs, ricotta and salt to form a dough ball. Add extra water as necessary to just help the ball come together. The dough should be the texture of semi firm play dough. Not too firm, but still soft.

2. Cut the 2 cup dough ball into 2 equal sized 1 cup dough balls. Wrap one in plastic wrap and store in the freezer for later use if you only want to make a 1 cup batch. Otherwise, prepare both sections.

3. Cut 1 of the dough ball section into (4) 1/4 cup, then cut those in half into small 1/8 cup sections.

4. Roll each 1/8 section into long ropes, about as thick as your pinky finger. Lightly spray with cooking spray to help prevent sticking.

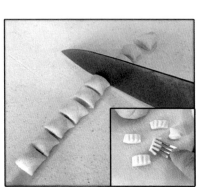

5. Cut each strand into small gnocchi. You should be able to get around 60-70 small gnocchi per 1/4 cup section. Then, lightly press down on each dumpling with a small fork, to give them a gnocchi "look" and make them slightly larger.

6. Drop dumplings into boiling water and cook for 2-3 minutes. Toss with your sauce immediately, or rinse with cold water and store in a ziplock bag in the fridge for later.

Pictured is 3 points of cooked, store bought lasagna noodles, next to 3 points of my cooked fresh pasta, made from a single 1/4 portion of dough. The fresh pasta sheet is approx. only 10 more calories, while being 3-4x the size.

This image shows the difference between 13 points of my cooked fresh linguini, next to 13 points of boiled, store bought spaghetti

- **No Pasta Maker? No Problem:**
  Though it's ideal to try and make pasta with a pasta maker, you CAN make it without one. Sure, the finished pasta isn't uniform, but you'll definitely get activity points in while making it. Use a rolling pin to roll out the 1/4 cup sections of dough to be as wide/long/thin as you can. It won't be as great as with a machine, but it's doable. Dust your flat-ish dough with a little flour, using the wire strainer trick, then gently roll it into a long pinwheel. Use a sharp knife to cut thin slices into the rolled up dough. Once opened up, they will be long noodles.

- **Minimize Points from Dusting:**
  When making your dough, try to not add too much liquid at once. Your goal is to have the dough just come together (for the regular pasta dough, not the gnocchi). Too wet, and you'll have to add more flour, which will up the points. As mentioned earlier, place 1-1/2 tsp of flour into a fine mesh wire strainer. If you HAVE to dust your dough, gently tap the strainer while holding it over your dough, so that it gets a very light dusting. That 1-1/2 tsp will last a long time this way. If the dough is a little too dry, spritz it with a light mist of olive oil cooking spray. Unlike water, it will add moisture while also helping it to avoid sticking.

- **Freezing Dough:**
  I mention freezing extra balls of dough. I'm usually asked how I freeze it and how long it lasts in the freezer. I wrap it in plastic wrap, then put that in a ziplock bag. I've thawed dough out 6 months later and used it. Haven't died yet. Wooot!

Low Point Crust

Replacing Traditional Graham Cracker Crusts for Pies

One of the hardest things to manage while trying to eat healthier is desserts. Let's face it, it's the biggest hurdle for most of us, we love our sweets. Chief among those is pie, traditionally made with a ton of crushed graham crackers, sugar and butter. Regular Graham Cracker pie crust is a freaking Calorie Bomb, and as such is a ton of points. A typical graham cracker pie crust for a 9" pie will add around 55-70 points to your recipe, making it virtually impossible to have pies without blowing through all of your dailies. Well, you can still have pie crust, you just have to get creative and make some compromises.

As with all of this weird stuff I stumble upon, it's all born out of a desire to continue eating the foods I want, period. So, who would know how to knock the points from sugar and butter out of a dessert? Diabetics. I started searching through Diabetic cooking sites and forums and saw that they tended to use low sugar, high fiber cereals for their pie crusts instead of graham crackers. Turns out those are a lot less points than graham crackers too. After a few attempts, this is what I came up with.

R D
1-1
Points for 1/8 section of crust

- last checked 11/15/22 -
Use your mobile device's 'Camera' App to look at this code for nutritional info.

Ingredients:

- 1-1/4 cups Fiber One cereal, Kelloggs All Bran, or other low point High Fiber cereal
- 2 sheets (8 crackers) Low Fat graham crackers
- 1/2 cup fat free plain Greek yogurt
- 3/4 tsp ground cinnamon
- 1 Tbsp **PLUS** 2 tsp sugar free maple syrup (pancake syrup)
- 6-8 second spray, butter flavored cooking spray ***
- 1/2 cup 0 point brown sugar replacement, such as:
  (truvia 0 calorie brown sugar substitute, swerve brown, etc.)

Directions:

1. Put the cereal and graham crackers in a food processor, process on high until the cereal is ground into crumbs,
2. Add the remaining ingredients, spray into the mixture with your cooking spray, then process until well combined.
3. Spray a 9" pie pan or springform pan with cooking spray.
4. Press mixture down into pie pan and compress slightly. with your hands & fingers.
5. Use the same as you would a regular graham cracker crust.

Servings:

- Yield: Makes enough crust for a 9 inch pie pan.
- 10 total points, if Greek yogurt is 0 points on your plan.
- The above listed points, assume 8 servings

COOKING TIPS:

- This crust is not as sweet as a regular graham cracker crusts. That's because regular graham crackers have enough sugar to make Paul Bunyan diabetic.
- You can also consider adding some additional flavorings with baking extracts, such as vanilla, caramel, maple, or even pumpkin pie spice extract.
- Want it a little softer? Add some baking powder. Want it a little crisper? Add some baking soda and a splash of apple cider vinegar.
- Low Fat graham crackers are lower in points and calories than regular graham crackers. This recipe uses 2 sheets of 'honey maid low fat cinnamon grahams'. 5 points in total.

Dairy Free Pudding

Ever asked in Connect, a cooking forum, message board, facebook group, wherever... "Can you make pudding with Almond Milk?" and been met with an immediately dismissive "NO! It's impossible! Even Einstein couldn't figure it out!" Well, forget those Negative Nancys, they have no idea what they're talking about. You can make instant pudding with ANYTHING. Heck, in all of my pudding based frostings, I use cold water... so BOOM *mic drop*. It's suuuuuper easy and is extremely useful for cutting points when you're creating a recipe. It's also great for shaving a few extra calories off. Remember, a few calories here and there, add up over time. Summer's coming up and'ya want to look good in that leopard print speedo or tankini don't you?

Points:

The points are COMPLETELY dependent on what brand of pudding you buy (SCAN THE BOX), what dairy free liquid you use, as well as your application for the pudding. IE: Using it in a pie, eating it plain, parfait, etc. This page is just showing you how to make it.

Ingredients:

- Any brand of **INSTANT** pudding and pie filling
- Half as much fat free liquid as box-requested whole milk
    - Almond, Cashew, Soy Milk, etc.
    - Even COLD water works

Directions:

This is a truly simple food hack. All that is really required is the ability to pour liquid, use an electric hand mixer... and do 3rd grade math, unless you learned Common Core. Then, this simple math would require knowledge of Astro Physics. For this example, we're going to make instant butterscotch pudding, using cold water. Yes... water.

2. Mix, on high speed, for around 2 to 3 minutes, until the pudding gets thick and creamy. Store in the fridge, allowing more time to set. Done.

Notes:

- Using 1/2 as much fat free liquid, as the suggested milk, makes it a creamy pudding consistency. If you plan to use it for frosting, you'll need to make it thicker. Use less than 1/2. IE: If the box calls for 2 cups of cold milk, use 3/4 cup of fat free liquid. If the box calls for 3 cups of milk, use 1-1/4 cups of fat free liquid. This will make a thicker pudding, which you can use for frosting.

1. In a mixing bowl or container, mix 1 packet of instant pudding and pie filling, with HALF AS MUCH water for the whole milk the instructions suggest. So for example, if the box says to use 3 cups of cold milk, use 1-1/2 cups of cold water or almond milk instead.

Slow Cooker Roasted Garlic

Easy "Roasted" Garlic in your Slow Cooker

For those of you who are just starting out in the kitchen, or if you just simply haven't tried it before, I hope that I can convert you to the glories of Roasted Garlic. Where regular raw garlic has a sharp bite to it, Roasted Garlic is Raw Garlic's cool cousin that pulls up riding a Harley and blasting "Born In The USA", before riding off with your girlfriend.... nerd. It has a deep flavor that is much smoother than regular garlic. Its "bite" is so mild that you can even eat it on its own, like macho candy, without flinching.

As a busy dad who has errands to run, roasting garlic in the oven isn't always practical, so doing it in the slow cooker is perfect. Throw a bunch of garlic in, come back 6 hours later, done.

Serving Info:
Yield: A bunch 'o garlic
Servings: n/a
Serving Size: n/a

Range:
No points on any plan, period.

What You'll Need:
- Slow Cooker
- Whole Heads of Raw Garlic, as many as you want
- Aluminum Foil Wrap
- Cooking Spray ***
- Pinch of Salt
- Commercial-grade gas mask (optional)

Directions:

1. On a cutting board, use a knife to cut off the top 1/4 to 1/2 inch (depending on size of the garlic) from the top of each head. Remove some of the flaky papery skin from around the garlic.

2. Make an aluminum foil pouch that's at least 2 layers thick (a large piece of foil folded in half, to help avoid burning) and large enough to contain all of the cut heads of garlic.

3. Spray 5 times into the pouch with the olive oil cooking spray, coating all of the heads in a thick layer, then close the foil pouch. Leave a small slit or two.

4. Place a small cup or dish on the bottom of your slow cooker, and then place your foil pouch on top of it to help reduce the chance of burning. Cover and cook on the LOW setting for 6 hours.

5. Remove Garlic from the slow cooker and allow it to cool on a cutting board until you can handle it with your bare fingers. Careful, it's hot. Squeeze the soft garlic out of the skins, and store in a plastic ziplock bag in the freezer. Break off a few cloves whenever you need some. They thaw very quickly once removed from the freezer.

Notes:

- You can also roast garlic in your oven. It's essentially the same process. Bake the foil-wrapped garlic at 400 degrees for 35-40 minutes. Done.

- I prefer to have my slow cooker make this in my back yard. If you cook this inside your house for 6 hours your house will smell like a pizza parlor for days.

- Studies have shown that roasting garlic in this manner helps to prevent Vampire nests from forming on/near your property.

- Eating lots of garlic has been shown to work as a repellent for unwanted harassment and physical advances.

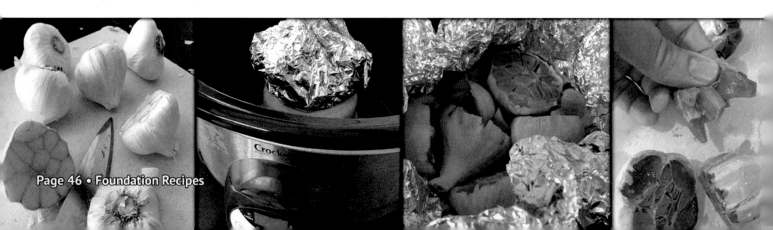

Baby, You So Spicy!

Toasting & Blooming Spices, Seeds and ..... Stuff

Though only 1 of the recipes in this cooking guide calls for toasting seeds or spices (Mexican Mole' sauce), this technique WILL be used in later cookbook volumes. Toasting spices and herbs enhances the flavors of some of my ground meat seasonings, as well as any of my sauces, dips and dressings that call for spices. You can toast whole spices, like fennel, caraway & coriander seeds. You can then use them whole, crush them, or you can buy an inexpensive spice grinder (I got mine for $8 on amazon) for fresh ground spices.

Aside from whole spices, you can "bloom" ground spices and even fresh herbs, like sprigs of rosemary and thyme. It's virtually the same process, but with ground spices and herbs. Other recipes, later on, will use toasted seeds, shredded coconut and more.

What You'll Need:

- A Pan
- Some Heat
- Seeds, Spices, Nuts, Herbs *(the legal kind, please)* and more
- A Fully Functioning Sniffer

Directions - Whole Spices:

1 Preheat a small pan over medium-low heat for around 30 seconds.
2 Add the amount of spices that you'll need into the pan. Shake it or stir the spices to prevent burning. Smaller spices and spices with thin skins need just a minute.
3 Once the spices become fragrant, remove them from the pan. If you plan to crush or grind your spices, allow them to cool first. Done.

Directions - Ground Spices (blooming):

1 Preheat a small pan over medium-low heat for around 30 seconds. For 0 point blooming, spray butter or olive oil cooking spray into the pan. Allow the spray to heat up a little bit, then add your ground spices to it and stir with a rubber spatula or wooden spoon, to form a paste. Lower the heat to low, ground spices can burn faster than whole.
2 Stir the spices to prevent burning. Once the paste become fragrant, add it to your dish.

Directions - Everything Else:

1 Pretty much the same as either of the above methods, just use common sense.
2 Use the "whole spice" method for toasting pine nuts, sesame seeds, peppercorns, wandering gnomes that you might find in your travels...

Note:

- You can add fresh sprigs of rosemary, thyme and other herbs to a hot pan to make them more fragrant, prior to adding them into a dish, though it does cause them to wilt slightly.
- Crush toasted seeds by placing them in a ziplock bag, then playing whack-a-mole with a kitchen mallet, a small pot, or a typical receipt from CVS Pharmacy.
- If you don't mind the extra points, you can use butter or oil to bloom your spices, but adjust your recipe's points accordingly.
- You can bloom ground spices without any oil, spray, or liquids. Add the ground spices to a hot pan and stir as you would whole spices. Keep an eye on them though, or they'll burn.

Slider Buns (Pretzel)

Moist, Soft, Fluffy, De-Freakin-Licious "Pretzel" Buns

This is a variation of my standard yeast burger bun (recipe on pg's 50-51). However, rather than baking these, we're first going to boil them, then bake them. That quick boil makes a HUGE difference with the texture, once baked. They end up tasting like a soft, doughy, chewy pretzel. Errrr-Ma-Gaaaawd, they are good!

Serving Info:

Yield: 8 slider buns
Servings: 8
Serving Size: 1 bun

R D
2-2

- last checked 11/15/22 -
Use your mobile device's 'Camera' App to look at this code for nutritional info.

Ingredients:

Egg Dough, Slider Buns

- 1 cup self rising flour
- 3 tsp sugar (2 tsp for yeast/water, 1 tsp in flour)
- 2 tsp active dry yeast (found in the baking/spice aisle)
- 1/4 cup very warm water (around 100 degrees)
- additional water, 3-4 Tbsp for mixing
- Cooking spray (i like butter flavored, but that's just me)
- 1 large egg + 1 tsp water for egg wash *(OPTIONAL)*

Water Bath

- big pot o' boiling water (Yup, pre-heat a big pot of water!)
- 1/4 cup baking soda (stir it into the water)

Directions:

1. Scoop the active dry yeast and 2 teaspoon of sugar, into a tall container or cup. Take 1/4 cup of aaaalmost hot water, around 100 degrees (ideally you want between 100-110. Too hot and the yeast dies too cold and it won't rise) and pour it into a tall cup, with the yeast. Stir the water gently to mix the ingredients, then allow to sit, untouched, for 10 minutes. It will foam up, a LOT.

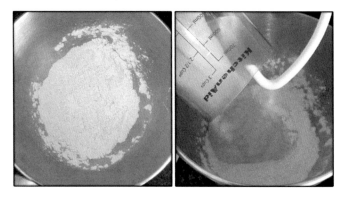

2. Place the flour and remaining 1 teaspoon of sugar into a large mixing bowl. After the yeast has "bloomed" for 10 minutes (pictured in step 1b), pour the yeast water into the flour.

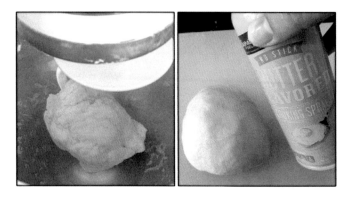

3. Begin mixing the dry and wet ingredients. The mixture will be dry and you'll need to add more warm water. It took me 3-4 additional Tablespoons of water for it all to JUST form a dough ball. You want the dough to require as little extra liquid as possible. Ideally, you want it to end up with the consistency of semi firm clay or 'play-doh'. If it's a little tacky, lightly spray it all with cooking spray, problem solved. Lightly spray a cutting board with cooking spray, then get to work.

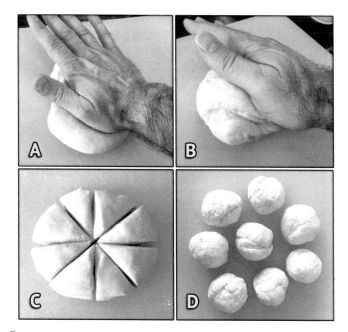

5. **(A)** Push down on the dough with your palm, then **(B)** fold the dough over and push down again. Repeat the folding process 20 times, then roll the dough back into a large ball. **(C)** Cut the ball into 8 equal sections, then **(D)** roll the cut sections into balls. Spray with cooking spray if the dough is tacky.

7. Lightly spray the top of each bun with butter flavored cooking spray then bake at 450 degrees for 13-16 minutes, or until the buns are dark brown. all around. Done.

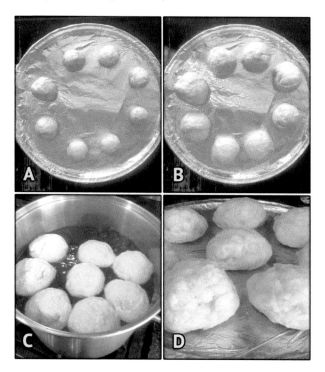

Pictured with my breakfast sausage patties, egg and country gravy

6. Preheat your oven to 450 degrees, for later.
   (A) Prep a baking pan with foil and cooking spray. Place the 8 dough balls onto the baking sheet, spaced apart, then gently press down on them, just a little bit, to flatten the tops slightly. Spray them with cooking spray. **(B)** Turn the heat back up on your pot of water, so it goes back up to a boil. Meanwhile, Let the dough balls rise for **ONLY** 10 minutes. **(C)** Carefully place all 8 dough balls into the boiling water. Boil for 30 seconds, then flip and boil for another 30 seconds. **(D)** Remove from the water, with a slotted spoon and return to your baking sheet.

Notes:
- If you are allergic to gluten, you can make this recipe with gluten free flour. Bob's Red Mill has a wide range of Gluten Free flours, that are available in many major supermarkets.
- To make regular sized buns, cut the 1 cup dough balls into three 1/3 dough balls. Let them rise for 15 minutes, rather than 10. Then boil and bake as directed, adjusting points for fewer servings.
- If you want your pretzel buns to have salt on top, sprinkle the tops with coarse kosher salt before they go in the oven.

Yeast Burger Buns

Homemade light, fluffy and deliciously low Point burger buns

This is my first TRUE success at perfectly sized and shaped burger buns. Unlike 2 ingredient dough, which ends up always tasting like a biscuit, these buns have a great texture, brown beautifully, taste like REAL BREAD and have a soft, light and fluffy interior. I know that a lot of us can buy 1-2 point 'keto' burger buns at our local stores, but not everyone has access to them, so these are a great option. Plus, they are homemade, so you know exactly what is in them... and what's in them is delicious.

Serving Info:

Yield: 4 buns
Servings: 4
Serving Size: 1 bun

R   D
3-3
AFTER scooping
bread out from the
top bun

To lower the listed Points by 1 point per bun...
SCOOP BREAD OUT OF THE TOP BUN! It lowers them by 1 point.
- last checked 11/15/22 -
Use your mobile device's 'Camera' App to
look at this code for nutritional info.

- 2-1/4 tsp active dry yeast
- 2 tsp granulated sugar (you can't use sweetener)
- 1/2 cup water (<u>MUST</u> be between 100-110 degrees)
- 1 cup PLUS 3 Tbsp all purpose flour
  Cooking Spray, flavored (butter, olive oil, whatever you want).
- 1/4 tsp olive, canola or vegetable oil
- 1/4 tsp salt
- 1/4 tsp baking powder
- additional water, as needed (1 tsp at a time)

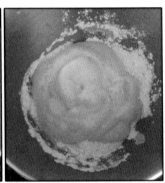

2. While the yeast is rising, Turn on your oven so that it preheats to 425 degrees. While it's heating up and your yeast is 'blooming', add the flour, salt and 1/4 tsp oil to a large mixing bowl. Spray into the bowl for 6 to 8 seconds (0 point amount, per your brand) of cooking spray. Then after the yeast has 'bloomed' for 15 minutes, pour the yeast-liquid into the bowl.

Directions:

1. Scoop the active dry yeast and sugar into a tall container or cup. I know it sounds food-snooty, but it's VERY important... stir in 1/2 cup of 100-110 degree water. Use a thermometer if you have one, you <u>need</u> it to be between 100-110 degrees. Stir the water gently till mixed, then allow to sit, untouched, for 15 minutes.

3. Begin mixing the dry and wet ingredients together. The mixture will be a bit wet, but that's ok. Use a rubber spatula to scrape down the sides and continue mixing. It will have the consistency of very thick brownie batter at this point. Just trust me.. If it's a little tacky, don't worry about it. Spritz a cutting board with a light mist of cooking spray then scoop the soft dough onto it. The dough will still be pretty wet. It's ok.

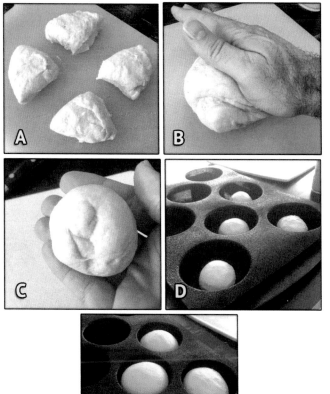

Notes:

- **_FORGOT TO MENTION!!!:_** I purchased an inexpensive rubber silicone "hamburger bun mold" on Amazon, to use for this recipe. This way, the dough forms, and bakes into a perfect hamburger bun shape. Get one with small perforations all around the cavities. Set the mold on a baking tray to use it.
- If you are allergic to gluten, you can make this recipe with gluten free flour. Bob's Red Mill has a really good Gluten Free '**_1 to 1 Baking Flour_**', that's available in many major supermarkets. Make sure to adjust your points, if necessary..
- You can use this recipe as a base and add your own flair to it. Add onions, garlic, cheddar cheese, sesame seeds, etc.
- If you don't have a mold, you can set the dough balls onto a baking pan and let them rise. However, it is a 'loose' dough. It won't take on the perfect shape of a burger bun, but that's ok. You're here to eat, not to make googly eyes at your buns... unless you're into that sorta thing. I won't judge.
- Double this recipe and rather than section it for buns, season the dough and use it for breadsticks. Look online for suggestions for cooking times with similar baked goods.
- **_POINTS!!!:_** If you build this recipe into the recipe builder, it will show the buns as being higher point as what I have listed. Here's why:

    Take your finished buns, which will be 4 points for the first bun, then <u>SCOOP OUT SOME BREAD</u> from the top bun! This will lower the points for 1 bun, from 4 points, to 3. This is all being done to make them a bigger, regular sized bun, while reducing them down from 4 to 3 points.

4. The dough will be pretty tacky and difficult to form, just spray it with a little cooking spray. It helps a lot.
   (A) Cut the ball into 4 equal sections, then **(B)** Gently fold each ball over itself about 15-20 times. **(C)** Roll the dough into a small ball in your palm. It will still be very very soft, that's what we want. **(D)** Place the seam side down, in the silicone mold, spray the top with cooking spray, then **(E)** walk away for 15 minutes. NO TOUCHING!

5. Bake the buns for 12-14 minutes, depending on how golden brown you want them to look. Remove from the oven, then.... trust me on this... put them in a bowl and cover it, or put them in a gallon sized ziplock bag. Let them 'steam', covered, for 5 minutes. It softens them and they take on a pillow softness. Right out of the oven they will have a hard crust, but resting, covered, will soften them up.

Yeast Pizza Dough

A Simple Airy & Crisp Yeast-Based Pizza Dough Recipe

A simple and basic Yeast-Based recipe that will let you make delicious thin or thick crust pizzas, calzones, baked bread bowls, bread sticks and much more. Making yeast dough sounds much more intimidating than it really is. It's great for when you will be home for a while and have some chores, or need to run errands away from the kitchen for an hour or two. It's great for a busy multi-tasking kinda day.

Ingredients:

- 1 cup All Purpose Flour (or your flour of choice)
- 1/4 tsp Salt (optional if on low sodium diet)
- 2-1/4 tsp Active Dry Yeast
- 2 tsp Sugar
- 1/2 cup Water, between 100-110 degrees
- cooking spray

Serving Info:

Yield: 1 batch
Servings: n/a
Serving Size: n/a

Listed points are for the ENTIRE pizza crust

- last checked 11/15/22 -
Use your mobile device's 'Camera' App to look at this code for nutritional info.

Directions:

1. Combine the flour and salt in a large mixing bowl. Set aside

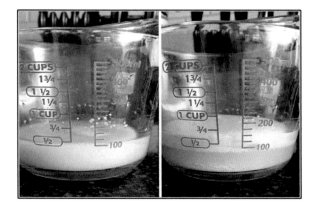

2. In another dish or cup, pour in the active dry yeast and sugar. Pour in the 1/2 cup of (not too hot) hot water then stir for a few seconds to mix. Allow the yeast water to sit untouched for 15 minutes. In that time the water will develop a frothy "head" to it.

3. After 15 minutes, pour the yeast mixture into the mixing bowl with the dry ingredients, then spray into the bowl for a few seconds with cooking spray. Mix to combine until a dough ball is formed, adding a bit more water if the mix is still too dry. It's ok if it's a little tacky.

4. Lightly spray a bowl with cooking spray and put the dough ball in, then cover the bowl with plastic wrap. Walk away and allow the dough to rise for 30 minutes. By that time, it will have expanded and fluffed up a bit.

5. Remove the dough and place it onto the center of a pizza pan that has been lightly sprayed with cooking spray. Stretch out the dough to a large round shape, spray the top with cooking spray and allow it to rest for 30 minutes, uncovered.

6. After 30 minutes the dough has risen a good deal, lightly spray the dough with olive oil cooking spray and gently stretch it more.

7. Put your sauce, cheese and toppings onto the pizza and start preheating your oven to 400 degrees.

8. After the oven has reached 400 degrees, which has given your pizza an additional 10-15 minutes to rise.... wipe the drool off your chin and get ready to bake some pizza.

9. Place your pizzza into the oven and bake at 400 degrees for 16-20 minutes. Ovens vary, so yours may take a different amount of time. Keep an eye on it, because, burned pizza sucks.

10. Bask in the glory of real pizza dough.

COOKING IDEAS:

- If you make a double batch of this dough you can make an AWESOME deep dish pizza in a 13"x9" casserole pan, using the exact same method listed to make this dough. Double all of the ingredients EXCEPT for the yeast. If you double the yeast, you'll be "tootin'"" the rest of the day.

- If you make a double batch you can also put your dough onto a large baking sheet pan rather than a round pizza pan, roll the dough into a long rectangular shape, then allow it to rise, stretch it more, rise, top it, bake it and you can get up to 18 good sized square slices out of it.

- You can use instant yeast instead of dry active yeast. Rather than adding the active dry yeast to water and waiting 10 minutes as stated in these directions, you can simply add 2-1/2 tsp of instant yeast directly into the flour with the warm water and mix the dough. It will rise when you let the dough ball rest. It saves a little time.

- You can use this to make Calzones, Strombolis, life sized edible statues of your pets... get creative.

- I personally like to add 1/2 tsp of garlic powder, 1/2 tsp of onion powder, 1 tsp of dried thyme and some cracked black pepper into the flour. The finished bread can be used as breadsticks or for paninis.

Black Peppercorn - pg 64

Parmesan Pomodoro - pg. 83

Pesto - pg. 84

**Asian Glaze - pg. 57
mixed with BBQ Sauce - pg. 60**

Sauce Recipes

This massive collection of low calorie, low fat, low sugar and low point sauces will help you "fancy up" any dish you want to serve. My sauces are created in such a way that you do NOT have to skimp on flavor or portion size to cut calories and lose (or maintain) weight. There's none of that ridiculous, "a serving size is 2 Tbsp" nonsense here. All of my sauces are either 1/4 or 1/2 cup and 0-1 points.

Chimichurri Sauce ... pg 69

(yeah, it's not a sauce, but you deserve Hummus)

Marsala Wine Sauce ... pg 81

Arrabbiata Sauce

DO NOT MAKE THIS SAUCE IF YOU CAN'T TOLERATE SPICY FOOD!

Are you one of those crazy people who's always loved spaghetti with marinara sauce, while also wondering what it'd be like to replace it with liquid magma? Well, boy, do I have a sauce for you!! Arrabbiata sauce means 'angry' sauce. Why angry? Because it'll melt your face off. I made mine with 3 tsp of red pepper flakes... so I'm currently waiting by the window, for the ambulance.

Ingredients:

- olive oil cooking spray, 6-8 second spray
- 1 cup diced onion
- 4 medium garlic cloves, crushed and minced
- 2 to 3 tsp crushed red pepper flakes
- 3 Tbsp white wine (or chicken broth, you do you)
- 45 oz canned, crushed tomatoes (I used (1) 30 oz and (1) 15 oz can.
- 2 Tbsp italian seasoning
- 1 tsp 0 point sweetener o' choice
- 1/2 tsp salt

Serving Info.:

Yields: 5-1/2 cups
Servings: 5 (plus change)
Serving Size: 1 cup

- last checked 11/15/22 -
Use your mobile device's 'Camera' App to
look at this code for nutritional info.

Directions:

1. Heat a medium sized pot over medium heat. Spray with olive oil cooking spray, then add the onions, garlic and red pepper flakes. Cook for 3-4 minutes, till onions soften.
2. Pour in the wine (or broth) and cook for 2 minutes, till liquid is reduced by half.
3. Add the crushed tomatoes, Italian seasoning, sweetener and salt. Mix till well combined.
4. Bring to a boil, then reduce heat to medium-low and simmer for 20 minutes. Done.

Notes:

- THIS SAUCE IS SPICY!!!!!: If you can't tolerate spicy food, do not make this. Translated in Italian, the name of this sauce means "Angry". It's supposed to be hot.
- As mentioned, if you don't want to use wine, replace it with fat free chicken, beef or veggie broth.
- This sauce is meant to have some texture to it, so <u>do not</u> use canned tomato <u>sauce</u> or tomato <u>puree</u>. You are SUPPOSED to use canned, <u>crushed tomatoes</u>.
- Don't want to use sweetener? Fine, use sugar, but adjust what'cha need to.

Asian Glaze & Dipping Sauce

A thick and sticky dipping sauce that's easily customizable

This is a very simple Asian inspired sauce that can easily be docked up with additional spices and flavorings for your own preferences. This sauce is yummy as listed, but can be kicked up a few notches by adding lemongrass, some lime juice, honey, sugar free bbq sauce, or any number of additional flavors.

Ingredients:

- 2 Tbsp PLUS 2 tsp reduced sodium soy sauce
- 1 Tbsp 0 point sweetener o' choice (monkfruit, stevia, etc)
- 1/4 tsp molasses**
- 1 medium garlic clove, minced (1tsp)
- 1/2 tsp fresh ginger, minced. OR 1/4 tsp ground ginger
- 2 Tbsp tomato sauce
- 1-1/2 Tbsp sugar free pancake syrup**
- 2 Tbsp rice vinegar
- 1-1/4 cups Water
- 4-1/2 tsp cornstarch (dissolved into the water)
- 1/2 tsp asian chili sauce, such as Huy Fong chili garlic Asian sauce, or Sriracha.

Serving Info:
Yield: 2 cups
Servings: 8
Serving Size: 1/4 cup

RECIPE INFO
R D
0-0

- last checked 11/15/22 -
Use your mobile device's 'Camera' App to
look at this code for nutritional info.

Directions:

1. Dissolve the cornstarch with the water, then heat ALL of the ingredients in a small pot, over medium-high heat, till boiling.
2. Reduce heat, continue cooking at a boil low boil for 3-4 minutes, till it begins to coat the back of a spoon.
3. Remove sauce from heat, pour into a bowl and set aside. It will thicken as it cools.
4. Stir sauce again after 5 minutes off of heat, serve warm or cold.

Notes:

- If you have access to 0 point brown sugar substitute, swap the 2 Tbsp of sweetener and 1/4 tsp of molasses, with 2 Tbsp of 0 point brown sugar substitute.
- If you don't want to buy rice vinegar, use regular distilled white vinegar, it'll work just fine and still tastes great.
- Adding 1/4 tsp of sesame oil REALLY kicks the sauce up, without adding any points.

Avocado Cilantro Sauce

A deliciously creamy sauce perfect for meats, veggies and even salads

This velvety smooth avocado dressing is a tasty mix of herbs, creaminess, citrus and savoriness. It is just at home on tacos and fish as it is being used for a salad dressing. This is an extremely simple sauce because all that is required is a food processor or a large blender to puree the mixture. The reason we're able to get an entire 1/4 cup serving of this Avocado sauce for 1 point is that we are being smart with our ingredients. We're stretching out the Avocado with water, broth and greek yogurt to get a lot more servings out of it which decreases the points per serving.

The end result is a sauce that is creamy and smooth with a subtle lime flavor, a healthy dose of cilantro and a delicious richness from the Avocado.

Serving Info.:

YIELDS: 2-1/2 cups
Servings: 10
Serving Size: 1/4 cup

R D
1-1

- last checked 11/15/22 -
Use your mobile device's 'Camera' App to look at this code for nutritional info.

Ingredients:

- 1 medium Avocado
- 2 medium garlic cloves
- 1 cup fresh cilantro
- 3 Tbsp lime juice
- 1/2 cup water
- 1/2 cup fat free chicken broth
- 1 cup plain fat free greek yogurt
- 1/2 tsp salt
- 1/4 tsp pepper
- 1/4 tsp olive oil (get a bottle that says 'strong' or 'robust' flavor, if possible)

Directions:

1. Carefully slice the avocado in half, remove the pit and skin, then place the avocado into the food processor.
2. Add all of the remaining ingredients to the food processor and then puree on high speed for around 1 minute, or until the ingredients are broken down and smooth.
3. Season with additional salt and pepper, if necessary.
4. Serve immediately or chill in the refrigerator.

Notes:

- This is more of a savory sauce than a bright citrus one. If you would prefer it to have a less savory taste, then replace the chicken broth with additional water. Do not add any pepper, and only season with a minimal amount of salt, to taste, after the rest of the ingredients are finished being pureed.
- Add more water to thin the mixture, if you want a thinner sauce/dressing
- Because this recipe uses such a small amount of olive oil, I highly recommend buying a bottle that says 'robust' flavor or other word to denote a bold olive oil flavor.

Bang Bang Sauce

A creamy and INSANELY SPICY dipping sauce, for you weirdos that like that kinda stuff

For about 2 years now, people have been begging me to make a copycat version of 'The Bonefish Grill's' Bang Bang sauce. Having never been there, I was always "meh" about it. But, I decided I'd add it, since I'm revising this cookbook anyways. I just made it 1 hour ago and all I can say is... "Who in the heck eats this stuff!!!" This is like going to Hawaii, walking up to an active volcano, then leaning down and lapping up a mouthful of magma. I'm sure you folks who like spicy food will taste nuances in the sauce... but all I can taste is my tongue melting. Some of ya'll are crazy.

Ingredients:

- 1 cup plain fat free Greek yogurt
- 1 Tbsp light mayonnaise
- 4 Tbsp Asian chili sauce, I used Huy Fong chili garlic sauce.
- 1 tsp sriracha hot sauce.. because.. why not!?
- 1 Tbsp rice vinegar
- 1-1/2 Tbsp sugar free syrup (pancake)
- 2 Tbsp 0 point sugar replacement o' choice

Serving Info:

Yield: 1-1/4 cup
Servings: 5
Serving Size: 1/4 cup

RECIPE INFO

R D
0-1

- last checked 11/15/22 -
Use your mobile device's 'Camera' App to look at this code for nutritional info.

Directions:

1. Add all of the ingredients into a bowl, whisk together till combined. Cover and set aside. It's tasty as is, but the flavors develop the longer it sits.
2. I'd recommend having a fire extinguisher handy, for when your face decides to spontaneously combust.

Notes:

- If you don't want to use mayonnaise, feel free to replace it with an extra Tablespoon of Greek, it'll still taste like fire.... but, it'll remove 1 ingredient point from the recipe.
- Make sure to use an Asian chili sauce that is 0 points. 'Sweet' chili sauces have points from the added sugars. Regular copycat recipes call for using sweet chili sauce. Instead, I'm using 0 point Asian chili sauce and adding sweetener, to mimic the flavor.

Barbecue Sauce

A simple sauce that you can easily modify and build off of

Brush this simple sugar free barbecue sauce on chops, kebabs or chicken drumsticks before cooking, or use as a glaze during grilling. Serve it as either a hot or cold sauce to go with any of your favorite dishes. It's a perfect base to dock up yourself for a low point bbq style sauce. It's so low in points that you have a lot of room to play around with adding ingredients to make it your own.

Ingredients:

- 1/4 cup water
- 1 large onions, chopped
- 4 garlic cloves, medium, chopped
- 1 (29oz) can of tomato sauce (the 0 point kind)
- 1/3 cup worcestershire sauce
- 1/3 cup apple cider vinegar
- 1/4 cup sugar free syrup (pancake syrup)
- 1/3 cup 0 calorie brown sugar substitute
- 2 tsp ground mustard
- 1/2 tsp onion powder
- 1/2 to 3/4 tsp chili powder, to taste
- 2 tsp smoked paprika
- 2 tsp paprika
- 1/2 tsp liquid smoke, hickory (OPTIONAL)
- additional salt and pepper to taste
- (optional) 1 Tbsp lower sodium soy sauce

Serving Info.:

Yields: 5 cups
Servings: 10
Serving Size: 1/2 cup

R D
0-0

- last checked 11/15/22 -
Use your mobile device's 'Camera' App to look at this code for nutritional info.

Directions:

1 In a medium saucepan, saute the onions and garlic with cooking spray, until softened.
2 Stir in all of the remaining ingredients and heat to a low simmer.
3 Cover and simmer for 15 minutes.
4 Pour the mixture into a blender or food processor and process on high until smooth.
5 Return the sauce to the pan and season with additional salt and pepper, if desired.

Notes:

- This recipe is so low in points that it leaves you a lot of room to customize it.
- Want a southwest kick? Add 1 canned chipotle pepper in adobo sauce prior to pureeing, as well as a dash of McCormick's Chipotle Chili Powder. It adds some nice heat and a deep smoky flavor.
- Want an Asian version? Ditch the chili powder, then replace it with 1/2 tsp ground ginger. Add a total of 3-1/2 Tbsp lower sodium soy sauce... as well as 1 tsp sesame oil. Adjust your points.
- Don't want to buy brown sugar replacement? Use regular sweetener, it'll still taste fine.

Bearnaise Sauce

A Classic French Herbed Wine Sauce For Meat Eaters

A classic French sauce gets a low point makeover in this lightened version of one of the most classic French "mother" sauces. Typically, it is made with an emulsion of egg yolk, white wine, vinegar, herbs and loooots of butter. This sauce is Hollandaise's sophisticated wine drinking older brother.

Ingredients:

- 5 Tbsp white wine vinegar
- 1 Tbsp white wine, chardonnay
- 1 cup water
- 1 small onion, chopped
- 6-8 second spray, butter flavored cooking spray ***
- 1 bay leaf
- a few sprigs each of fresh parsley and tarragon
- 1/4 tsp cracked black pepper
- 1-1/2 Tbsp I Can't Believe It's Not Butter, Light
- 1-1/2 tsp cornstarch, dissolved in a little bit of water, set aside
- 3 large egg yolks
- 1 Tbsp finely chopped fresh parsley
- 1 Tbsp finely chopped fresh tarragon

Serving Info.:

Yields: 2 cups
Servings: 8
Serving Size: 1/4 cups

RECIPE INFO   R D
              0-0

- last checked 11/15/22 -
Use your mobile device's 'Camera' App to
look at this code for nutritional info.

Directions:

1. Combine the white wine, vinegar, water, chopped onion, bay leaf, pepper, butter spray, butter spread and the sprigs of fresh herbs in a small stock pot and heat until boiling. Lower the heat to medium/low and keep at a low simmer for 5 minutes.

2. Pour the mixture through a wire strainer and into a bowl, to remove all of the vegetables and herbs. Set the bowl of strained liquid aside and allow to cool for 30 minutes.

3. After cooling for 30 minutes, return the mixture to your sauce pot and whisk in the egg yolks and dissolved cornstarch. Turn on the stove to medium and heat until the sauce begins to warm and thicken, about 5 minutes, stirring with a rubber spatula.

4. Once the sauce comes to a low simmer, reduce the heat to barely simmering and allow to continue cooking for 3 minutes, continue stirring.

5. Pour the thickened sauce into a bowl and stir in the chopped fresh parsley and tarragon. Can be served as a hot or cold sauce.

Bechamel Sauce

A deliciously light and versatile take on a classic French sauce

Bechamel is a creamy base sauce, typically loaded with heavy cream and butter. We are using unsweetened almond milk and I can't believe it's not butter Light, cooked with vegetables and herbs to create a simple sauce with a subtle depth of flavor. It has an excellent mellow base, which makes it ideal for lasagnas, as well as an accompaniment for many fish, egg, and vegetable dishes. It can also be used as a base in a wide range of sauces and dishes. Add some garlic and you have a creamy garlic sauce, add lemon and herbs and you have a creamy lemon and herb sauce, the possibilities are endless. I personally like to use it for the white sauce in my low-ish point chicken and vegetable lasagna. It's a much healthier WW-ified take on a major brand's frozen vegetable lasagna that we all know and love...which rhymes with 'Stopherz'.

Ingredients:

- 1/2 cup unsweetened almond milk
- 3 cups water
- 1 Tbsp I can't believe it's not butter Light
- Butter flavored cooking spray, 5-6 seconds spray ***
- 1 tsp chicken flavored bouillon (granules)
- 1 pinch of nutmeg
- 2-3 sprigs of fresh parsley
- 2-3 sprigs of fresh rosemary or thyme
- 1 small onion, chopped
- 1 medium carrot, peeled and chopped
- 1 celery stalk, chopped
- 1 bay leaf
- 1/4 cup plain fat free Greek yogurt
- 4 Tbsp cornstarch, mixed into the Greek yogurt
- 1/2 tsp salt
- black or white pepper, to taste

Servings:

Makes: 3 cups
Servings: 12
Serving Size: 1/4 cup

R D
0-1

- last checked 11/15/22 -
Use your mobile device's 'Camera' App to look at this code for nutritional info.

Notes:

- Use any type of butter you want, but adjust points accordingly. I am using 1 point of I can't believe it's not butter Light, in this recipe.
- If you would prefer to use actual broth instead of the chicken flavored granules, leave out the granules/bouillon and replace 1 cup of the water with 1 cup of fat free chicken or vegetable broth.

Directions:

1. Dice the onion, carrot and celery. Spray a medium stock pot with the butter flavored cooking spray and cook the veggies on medium heat for 3-4 minutes, until they begin to sweat.
2. Pour in the water, milk, butter spread, bouillon, nutmeg, along with the salt, fresh herbs and bay leaf. Bring to a boil, over medium heat, then remove the pot from the heat and allow the mixture to steep for 30 minutes.
3. Pour the cooled mixture through a strainer, into a bowl, to remove the vegetables and herbs.
4. In a separate bowl, combine the cornstarch and yogurt until smooth, adding a little bit of the sauce to warm up the Greek.
5. Pour the strained liquid back into the pot and stir in the yogurt/cornstarch mixture, until smooth.
6. Heat the mixture over medium heat, stirring frequently, until it reaches a low boil. Reduce the heat and allow to barely simmer for 3-4 minutes for the sauce to thicken up a bit.
7. Remove the pan from the heat and season to taste with pepper.
8. The sauce can be served immediately, or it can be allowed to cool for a few minutes. It thickens more as it cools.

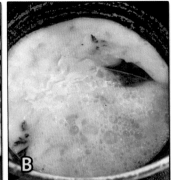

NOTE: All Bechamel variation recipes have the same 1/4 cup serving size as the original bechamel sauce.

Bechamel Variations

Bechamel is a perfect base for a number of creamy, savory sauces. You can make 1 batch of Bechamel and easily modify it for your own tastes with just a few minor tweaks. For all of these sauces, make a regular batch of Bechamel sauce with the listed changes and additions. This'll show you how easy it is to make your own creations.

Alfredo Sauce:

Recipe Changes:

R D
1-1

Use your mobile device's 'Camera' App to look at this code for nutritional info.

- Add *3 chopped cloves of garlic* to the vegetables in the first step of the Bechamel sauce.
- Stir in *4-1/2 Tbsp of reduced fat Parmesan grated topping*. (such as Kraft reduced fat Parmesan)

- last checked 11/15/22 -

Lemon & Chive Cream Sauce:

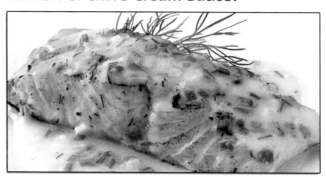

Recipe Changes:

R D
0-1

Use your mobile device's 'Camera' App to look at this code for nutritional info.

- Use a small bunch of chopped *fresh chives* <u>in place of</u> the Rosemary or Thyme during the first steps of making your Bechamel sauce. Strain as normal.
- Add *2 Tbsp of lemon juice* to the sauce
- *3 Tbsp fresh chopped* to the finished sauce, as garnish.

- last checked 11/15/22 -

Creamy Herb Sauce:

Prepared by: @ mugglemama2017

Tarragon Sage Chicken with Butternut Squash Soup and Tarragon Sage Cream

Recipe Changes:

R D
0-1

Use your mobile device's 'Camera' App to look at this code for nutritional info.

- Replace the rosemary or thyme in the Bechamel sauce *with any other herb*, such as dill, tarragon, sage, basil, cilantro, etc. and remove during straining.
- Stir in more finely chopped fresh herbs to the sauce at step 7, when it is completely finished cooking and removed from heat, as garnish.

- last checked 11/15/22 -

Roasted Garlic Cream Sauce:

Recipe Changes:

R D
1-1

Use your mobile device's 'Camera' App to look at this code for nutritional info.

Add *5-6 medium sized cloves of roasted garlic* (pg 46) to all of the vegetables when making the Bechamel. Also, add *1-1/2 tsp garlic powder* and *2 Tbsp reduced fat grated parmesan topping* (like Kraft parmesan topping). Strain out the garlic cloves along with the other vegetables.

- last checked 11/15/22 -

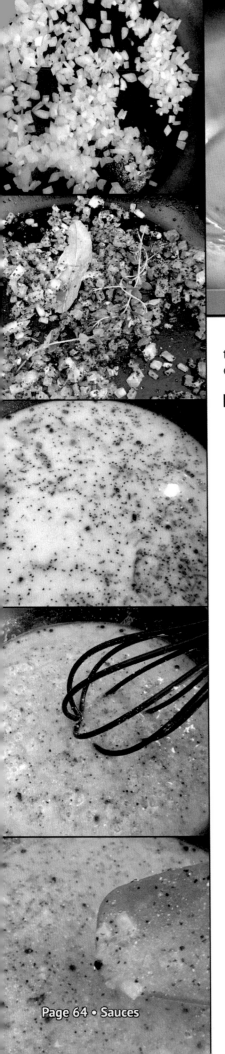

Black Peppercorn Sauce

A smoky black pepper cream sauce with delicious depth

This sauce tastes so good! It has a savory herbed butter flavor with a smoky pepperiness that sneaks up and karate chops the back of your tongue like an angry creamy ninja. It's great on beef and pork. Heck, it'd be good as lip balm for goodness sake.

Ingredients:

- 1 Tbsp I Can't Believe It's Not Butter Light
- 1 small onion, finely diced
- 2 medium garlic cloves, crushed and finely chopped
- 1/2 tsp salt
- 5 sprays, butter flavored cooking spray ***
- 1 bay leaf
- 3-4 sprigs fresh thyme
- 2-1/2 tsp black pepper ('coarse ground' or 'cracked' if able)
- 2-1/2 tsp whole black peppercorns
- 1/2 cup unsweetened plain almond milk
- 4-1/2 tsp cornstarch (mixed into the water)
- 1/2 cup fat free chicken broth
- 3/4 cup water
- 2 tsp lemon juice

Serving Info.:

Yields: 2 cups
Servings: 4
Serving Size: 1/2 cups

- last checked 11/15/22 -
Use your mobile device's 'Camera' App to look at this code for nutritional info.

Directions:

1. Melt the butter spread in a pan and cook onions for 3-4 minutes, until sweating. Add the garlic and cook for 1-2 minutes, until it becomes fragrant.
2. Spray the onions and garlic for 5 seconds with butter flavored cooking spray, add the herbs, salt, black pepper and peppercorns to the pan. Cook on medium-low heat for 3-4 minutes.
3. In a separate bowl, whisk together the almond milk and cornstarch, then add the chicken broth, water and lemon juice.
4. Pour the liquid mixture into the pan with the onions and pepper, stir constantly with a whisk. Bring the sauce up to a low boil and continue stirring for 3-4 minutes, until it thickens to your desired consistency. Use a fork to remove and discard the thyme leaves and bay leaf.
5. Turn off the heat and serve immediately, or allow to cool for a few minutes. The sauce thickens more as it cools.

Notes:

- You can replace the almond milk with any type of milk you want, but adjust points accordingly.
- This would be great with sauteed mushrooms added into it, which would have the added benefit of "bulking up" the sauce. Doing so would not just taste great, but it would both increase the servings and possibly lower the points for the first serving.
- If you'd like to add a little bit more savory depth of flavor to the sauce, you can stir in up to 1-1/4 teaspoons of reduced fat parmesan topping (like Kraft) into the sauce, for 0 points.
- This recipe gets 1 ingredient point from peppercorns. Ignore that, if you don't count spices.

Bolognese & Ragu Sauces

An extremely hearty meat sauce originating from Bologna Italy

A traditional Bolognese sauce is a thing of beauty. Where a Marinara sauce is what you would typically think of when you picture a plate of spaghetti or on a pizza, a Bolognese sauce is much more hearty. The sauce is usually packed with ground beef or pork sausage, but we are going for a low fat, low calorie, low point sauce, so we are using my ultra low point, ultra flavorful 0 point italian sausage recipe from page 28. You can easily transform this into an equally delicious chunky ragu sauce, by tweaking the spices and not pureeing the vegetables. Want to make this even more filling? Add some mushrooms to get even more servings out of it.

Ingredients:

- 1 pound of **MY** turkey Italian Sausage, recipe on pg. 28
- 1 medium onion, diced (around 1-1/2 cups)
- 1/2 cup carrot, finely chopped***
- 1/2 cup celery, finely chopped***
- 4-5 medium garlic cloves, minced
- 2/3 cup fat free beef or chicken broth
- 1 Tbsp red wine vinegar
- 1/4 cup red wine
- 2 Tbsp tomato paste, no salt added
- 29 oz. canned tomato sauce (scan to ensure 0 points)
- 1/2 cup unsweetened plain almond milk **
- 1 tsp italian seasoning
- 1/2 tsp fresh rosemary, minced
- 1/2 tsp ground allspice**
- 1/2 tsp ground nutmeg**
- salt and pepper to taste

Directions: *(for Bolognese)*

1. Cook the onions, celery, carrots and garlic in a pot with olive oil cooking spray (a 0 point amount) for 5-6 minutes, until they begin to sweat.
2. Add the broth. Cook for 5-10 minutes, or until almost all of the liquid has reduced.
3. Add the raw "italian sausage" and cook till browned, breaking up the meat into small pieces, with a spoon.
4. Add the vinegar, wine, tomato paste, tomato sauce, almond milk, italian seasoning, rosemary, allspice and nutmeg. Bring to a boil.
5. Reduce to low heat, then cover with a lid and cook at a low simmer, **COVERED**, for 30 minutes. Season to taste.

Serving Info.:
Yields: 6 cups
Servings: 12
Serving Size: 1/2 cup

RECIPE INFO
R D
0-0

- last checked 11/15/22 -
Use your mobile device's 'Camera' App to look at this code for nutritional info.

NOTES:

- For a chunky Ragu sauce, DON'T puree the vegetables.. Also, remove the almond milk, allspice and nutmeg.
- If you're allergic to almond milk, use a low point 'milk' you can have, or use fat free beef broth. It'll add a lot of flavor..

Buffalo Sauce

An addictively spicy hot sauce that holds the universe together

Good old Buffalo sauce, a Holy Union between cayenne pepper-based hot sauce, vinegar and lots and lots and lots of butter. It's one of those things that everyone enjoys, but that most people trying to cut calories have to avoid because of the fat content. Well, that was true until the heavens opened, the clouds parted, choirs of angels started singing and I bestowed this virtually fat free gift upon you all. Pretty much every single "skinny" food blogger does the same exact carbon copy recipe of, "Mix hot sauce with a bucket of Greek yogurt to make Buffalo sauce, Yippie!" Sorry, Susie... Homey don't play that. I don't use Greek yogurt as a culinary crutch. Also, instead of using a bunch of butter, we're using a combination of butter flavored cooking spray, butter spread and a mix of broth, water and spices that are used in real buffalo sauce recipes.

Ingredients:

- 6 second spray, butter flavored cooking spray
- 1/2 cup fat free chicken broth
- 1/2 cup water
- 4-1/2 tsp cornstarch
- 3/4 cup Franks Red Hot Cayenne Pepper Sauce, Original
- 2 tsp worcestershire sauce
- 2 Tbsp white vinegar
- 1 Tbsp I can't believe it's not butter Light
- 1/4 garlic powder
- 2 Tbsp plain fat free Greek yogurt
- additional salt and pepper, to taste

Serving Info.:

Yields: 1-3/4 cups
Servings: 7
Serving Size: 1/4 cup

R D
0-0

- last checked 11/15/22 -
Use your mobile device's 'Camera' App to look at this code for nutritional info.

Directions:

1 Spray the butter flavored cooking spray into a small sauce pot, then add the water, broth and cornstarch. Mix till the cornstarch is dissolved.

2 Add the hot sauce, worcestershire, vinegar, butter spread and garlic powder. Cook over high heat until the sauce comes to a rolling boil, then lower the heat to medium. Cook at a low boil for 3 minutes.

3 Pour the sauce into a mixing bowl and allow to cool for 15 minutes.

4 Add the Greek yogurt, stir or whisk until the Greek yogurt has been completely incorporated into the sauce, without lumps. Taste, season with salt or pepper, if desired. The sauce will continue to thicken as it cools. Done.

Note:

- If you'd like this to be more of a thick, creamy dip than a sauce... stir in a bit more Greek yogurt. However adjust points if you're plan doesn't give you fat free Greek for 0 points.
- Allergic to dairy? Swap out the Greek for Tofu (*gasp* Ingredient swaps!!)

Butter Sauce Base

A WW-ified butter sauce that can be adjusted for any recipe

If there is one thing that you'd NEVER think you'd be having on Weight Watchers, chances are it's a low point butter sauce. C'mon, we're talking about using beautiful, golden, liquid fat, for goodness sake. However, as with most recipes in this guide/book, a little bit of messing with ingredient swaps, and a little trial and error, will work wonders for your cooking, as well as your waist line.

This butter sauce is a faaaaaantastic base for you to use as the foundation for a lot of sauces of your own making. You can add some herbs, wine, capers, a little reduced fat Parmesan, whatever you'd like. As it's written below, this sauce is very tasty, but it is tailor made for you to customize.

Ingredients:

- 4-5 seconds spray, butter flavored cooking spray ***
- 5 Tbsp I can't believe it's not butter Light
- 1-1/4 cup water
- 1/2 cup fat free chicken broth
- 4-1/2 tsp cornstarch, dissolved into water
- 1/8 tsp turmeric (optional, for deeper color)
- 1/8 tsp salt, or more to taste.
- 2 tsp butter flavored popcorn seasoning sprinkles (optional)

Serving Info.:

Yields: 2 cups
Servings: 8
Serving Size: 1/4 cup

- last checked 11/15/22 -
Use your mobile device's 'Camera' App to look at this code for nutritional info.

Directions:

1 Spray the cooking spray into a small stock pot, then melt the butter spread over medium heat.
2 Add the water/cornstarch, turmeric (if using), chicken broth, salt and butter flavored sprinkles, if using, into the pot. Stir till the cornstarch dissolves, then turn up the heat and bring to a boil.
3 Cook at a rolling boil for 4 minutes, remove from heat. Done.

Note:

- Though optional, the Turmeric gives a deep golden color to the butter sauce. If you would like your sauce to be a lighter yellow, don't add it.
- The sauce will continue to thicken as it cools.
- If you want to add even more of a butter punch, you can add butter flavored popcorn sprinkles or butter extract, from the baking/spice aisle, next to the vanilla extract.
- This sauce would go great as a butter base for other sauces, or for a dipping sauce for lobster, crab, etc.

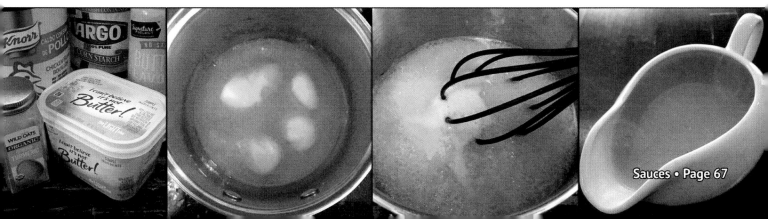

Cheese Sauce

A deliciously low point cheddar cheese base sauce

This page is devoted to all of you cheese heads out there. This is a very easy to make cheese sauce that is awesome on pretty much anything. It can be poured over a baked potato, tossed with pasta to make low point mac n cheese, the possibilities are pretty much endless. It's also extremely customizable and easy to dock up. This isn't as thick and goopy as canned cheese goop. This is slightly thinner, with the viscosity of hot nacho cheese.

Servings Info.:

Yields: 3-1/4 cups
Servings: 13
Serving Size: 1/4 cup

R   D
1-1

RECIPE INFO

- last checked 11/15/22 -
Use your mobile device's 'Camera' App to look at this code for nutritional info.

Ingredients:

- 2-1/4 cups water
- (1) 10-3/4oz can Campbell's "Healthy Request" Condensed Cheddar Cheese Soup.
- 1/2 tsp salt
- 1/2 tsp chicken flavored bouillon granules
- 1/8 tsp ground turmeric
- 2 tsp 'cheese' flavored popcorn seasoning sprinkles (I used 'Kernel Season's' brand, available at most major stores and walmarts.)
- 2 slices velveeta original cheese slices
- 4-1/2 tsp cornstarch, dissolved into the water

Directions:

1. In a medium sauce pot, stir together all of the ingredients, with a whisk, till the cornstarch dissolves. Turn on the heat and bring to a rolling boil. Lower the heat to keep the mixture at a rolling boil, without letting the sauce bubble over. Allow to cook at low boil for 5-6 minutes.
2. After 5-6 minutes, remove pot from heat and allow to cool for 10 minutes. The sauce will thicken slightly while it cools. Done

Notes:

- If your local store sells "Borden's" brand, fat free cheddar slices, use those instead of Velveeta. You can use 5 slices for 3 points, instead of Velveeta's 2 slices!!!
- You can substitue 1 cup of water with 1 cup of fat free chicken broth, if you don't want to use the chicken flavored bouillon granules.
- For Nacho Cheese sauce, use cayenne pepper for plain ol' heat. Adding chipotle chili powder (McCormick's) adds a little smokiness as well as heat.
- 1 can of the condensed soup shows as more points in the recipe builder. However, if you remove the soup from the can and do the points according to the weight and ACTUAL volume of the can's contents, it is lower in points.
- For an even thicker, really goopy Nacho Cheese sauce, you can add up to 1 additional tablespoon of cornstarch and still keep the first serving at 1 point.

Chimichurri Sauce

Pesto's Argentinian Cousin. Bold, Vibrant and With A Spicy Latin Punch

Chimichurri is one of those sauces that once you have it, you'll never forget it. Think of it like an Italian Pesto. A pesto that left its family and ran away to South America to join a violent street gang. Where Pesto is loaded with tons of fresh basil and parmesan, chimichurri is loaded with cilantro, parsley, lemon juice, vinegar and a good amount of heat from red pepper flakes. I'm making it healthier, by using a mixture of olive oil and water.

Ingredients:

- 2 cups fresh flat leaf (Italian) parsley, chopped, packed
- 2 cups fresh cilantro, chopped, packed
- 3 Tbsp capers, drained
- 4 medium garlic cloves
- 2 Tbsp red onion, finely diced
- 5 Tbsp red wine vinegar
- 3 Tbsp lime juice (or lemon, your preference)
- 1/2 tsp salt (or more, to taste)
- 1/8 to 1/4 red pepper flakes, to taste
- 1/4 tsp cracked black pepper
- 1/2 tsp fresh oregano (or 1/8 tsp dried)
- 2 Tbsp PLUS 1-1/2 tsp 'robust' olive oil (see notes)
- 6 second spray, olive oil cooking spray
- 1 cup room temperature water

Servings:

Yields: 2-1/4 cups
Servings: 9
Serving Size: 1/4 cup

RECIPE INFO   R D
1-1

- last checked 11/15/22 -
Use your mobile device's 'Camera' App to look at this code for nutritional info.

Directions:

1. Place all of the ingredients into a food processor. Spray the olive oil cooking spray into the processor, over the ingredients, then close the lid.
2. Pulse the food processor, to begin breaking down the leafy herbs. While pulsing, drizzle in the olive oil. Rememer, we don't want PUREE, we want it broken down.
3. Set aside, in the refrigerator and let the flavors meld for at least 1-2 hours.

NOTE:

- Because my recipe uses such a small amount of olive oil, I'd suggest buying regular olive oil, not extra virgin. Get one that says 'robust', 'extra flavorful', or an equivalent phrase denoting a strong flavor.
- Thogh the flavors taste more mellow/developed after 1-2 hours, the longer it sits the better.

Cilantro Lime Sauce

A simple and zesty sauce that packs some Latin attitude

This sauce is so simple and comes together so quickly that it'll come as a total surprise the first time that you make it. The flavorful mix of chicken broth, lime juice, garlic, and a bunch of fresh cilantro makes this an incredibly savory sauce. It punches you in the face with a nice bit of lime, followed by a strong flavor of cilantro. It pairs very well with Latin themed dishes, served over fish, chicken, beef and heck, even cardboard would taste great slathered in this stuff.

Though I'm using I Can't Believe It's Not Butter Light in this recipe, I give directions in the notes at the bottom of the page for how to make it a 0 point sauce with 1 simple ingredient substitution.

Serving Info.:
YIELDS: 1-1/2 cups
Servings: 6
Serving Size: 1/4 cup

R D
0-0

- last checked 11/15/22 -
Use your mobile device's 'Camera' App to
look at this code for nutritional info.

Ingredients:

- 5 second spray, olive oil flavored cooking spray ***
- 1 cup fat free chicken broth
- 1/4 cup water
- 4 tsp cornstarch, dissolved into the water
- 1/4 tsp olive oil
- 3 Tbsp lime juice
- 2-3 medium garlic cloves, crushed, chopped
- 1 Tbsp I can't believe it's not butter Light
- 3/4 cup cilantro (about 1 bunch), finely chopped
- salt and pepper to taste

Directions:

1 Spray the bottom of a medium pan with the cooking spray, then add the broth, water, cornstarch, olive oil, lime juice and garlic. Stir until the cornstarch is dissolved.
2 Add the butter spread, then turn on the stove and bring the sauce to a low boil, stirring to melt the butter spread.
3 Cook the sauce for 3-4 minutes at a rolling boil, until it begins to thicken, then turn off the heat and stir in the fresh chopped cilantro. Done.

Notes:

- Want even more butter flavor? Stir in 2 tsp of butter flavored popcorn seasoning sprinkles. Most all brands let you have 2 tsp for 0 points,
- Yes... you can seriously use an entire cup of this sauce for 1 point. Would you ever have an entire cup of sauce? No. But, that gives you a LOT of wiggle room to add points and customize this sauce for your own tastes. Add a point of this, a point of that... that's one of the reasons I make everything so low. It tastes good as-is, but you have room to modify my sauces.

Clam Sauce

A classic seafood sauce that's usually drenched in points

Ingredients:

- 6 second spray, butter flavored cooking spray
- 1 Tbsp I can't believe it's not butter Light
- 1/4 cup white wine, chardonnay
- 1 cups bottled clam juice, strained
- 1 cup fat free chicken broth
- 1/4 cup unsweetened almond milk
- 1 pinch red pepper flakes
- 5 garlic cloves, crushed, chopped
- 1 small onion, diced
- 2 (6oz) cans clams, minced or chopped
- 2 Tbsp oregano, finely chopped
- 2 Tbsp parsley, finely chopped
- 3-1/2 Tbsp cornstarch
- 1/4 tsp olive oil

Linguini with White Clam Sauce is one of those staples of traditional southern italian cooking. It's one of those dishes that we all love or have wanted to try, but we shy away from it because of how much wine and butter are typically in it. After a member on Connect requested that I take a look at WW-ifying it, I was able to come up with an ultra low point, low calorie, virtually fat free version that is light, delicious and extremely flavorful. Not to mention that it's 1 point for a REALISTIC portion size, not 2 points for 2 measly little Tablespoons of sauce like you'll find elsewhere.

Servings:
- Yield: 4 cups
- Servings: 8
- Serving Size: 1/2 cup

RECIPE INFO

R D
1-1

- last checked 11/15/22 -
Use your mobile device's 'Camera' App to look at this code for nutritional info.

Directions:

1 Spray the cooking spray into a medium pot, then add the butter spread, wine, broth, almond milk, clam juice, pepper flakes, garlic, diced onion and cornstarch. Stir until the cornstarch is dissolved, then bring the sauce to a rolling boil. Cook for 5 minutes, uncovered.

2 Turn off the heat. Pour in the contents of the 2 cans of canned clams and their juices. Add the chopped fresh herbs and finally, drizzle in the 1/4 tsp of olive oil. Season with salt, black (or white) pepper, and additional red pepper flakes, if desired.

Notes:

- Add 2 cups of canned, crushed or diced tomatoes and juices in place of the recipe's listed chicken broth, to create *"Clams and Tomato Sauce"*, a classic Neapolitan dish.
- Want even more 0 point butter flavor? Use 2 tsp of butter flavored popcorn seasoning sprinkles.
- If you REEEEALLY want to snazzy this dish up, add some live clams (scrub them clean!) to the pot and cook for 10 minutes. Discard any clams whose shells don't open.

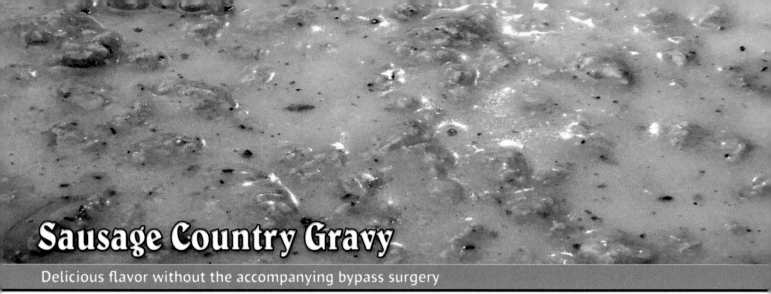

Sausage Country Gravy

Delicious flavor without the accompanying bypass surgery

This WW-ified country gravy isn't traditional. It's also not prepared by a grumpy line cook, at a truck stop, with a half pound of bacon grease on his apron. This is an incredibly low fat, low calorie version that still has a TON of flavor. Instead of full fat pork sausage, we are using my low fat, healthy, breakfast sausage from page 27. Instead of heavy cream and a mountain of fat, we're going to use almond milk, pan drippings and thickening it all with cornstarch.

Serving Size:
Yields: 5 cups
Servings: (10) 1/2 cup

RECIPE INFO

R D
1-1

- last checked 11/15/22 -
Use your mobile device's 'Camera' App to look at this code for nutritional info.

Ingredients:

Breakfast Sausage:
- 1 pound of **MY** turkey breakfast sausage, raw. Recipe on page 25.

"City Boy" Country Gravy
- 6 second spray, butter flavored cooking spray ***
- 1 Tbsp PLUS 2 tsp I Can't Believe It's Not Butter Light
- 2 cups unsweetened plain almond milk (not Vanilla!)
- 1 cup water
- 4-1/2 Tbsp cornstarch
- 3/4 tsp salt
- 1/2 to 1 tsp coarse ground black pepper to taste

Directions:

1. Prepare a batch of my ground turkey breakfast sausage ahead of time. Heat a large pan or a good sized pot, then cook the sausage, using cooking spray.. Break up the meat into small pieces, while cooking.
2. When the meat is cooked through, spray the butter flavored cooking spray onto the meat and mix in the butter spread. Heat till the butter spread is melted into the meat.
3. In a mixing bowl, combine the almond milk, water, cornstarch and pepper, until well combined, set aside.
4. Once the pan gets hotter than Ryan Gosling at your front door telling you "Hey girl, let me in... I'm here to vacuum and do your laundry.".... Pour the liquid mixture into the hot pan and start stirring. It should begin to thicken almost immediately.

5. Continue to stir on high heat, allowing the sauce to thicken for another minute or two, until it gets to a nice gravy consistency.
6. Turn off heat and season with salt and additional pepper, if desired. Don't skimp on the black pepper, because it REALLY makes the sauce taste authentic.

NOTE:
- If you're allergic to almond milk, you can use any similar low point beverage, just adjust your points. Carbmaster brand Lactose free milk at Kroger affiliated stores, is thick, low point, lactose free milk, that has the same thickness as almond milk and is also only 1 point per cup.
- I AM NOT PROVIDING A BISCUIT RECIPE!!! This is a recipe for the sauce only. Use any low point biscuit you want
- This does NOT look like goopy white country gravy, like you're used to ordering. THAT stuff is white because it is simply RENDERED FAT and TONS OF FLOUR. It gets it's white color from all the flour. Mine has neither.
- For a deeper flavor, swap the water for FF chicken broth

Creamy Horseradish Sauce

A Creamy, Zesty Sauce with More Kick Than A Mule

There's nothing quite like a good, creamy horseradish sauce. It's slightly spicy 'zing' cuts through fatty cuts of meat, while also managing not to completely overpower more mild proteins, such as chicken or fish. Where most recipes call for tons of full fat mayo or sour cream, I'm using fat free Greek as my cream-base. If you'd like to have a slightly spicier sauce, add a few dashes of your favorite hot sauce.

Ingredients:

- 1 cup plain fat free Greek yogurt
- 1/4 cup 'prepared' horseradish (see notes)
- 1 tsp light mayonnaise
- 1 Tbsp dijon mustard
- 1 tsp white wine vinegar OR lemon juice
- 1/2 tsp salt
- 1/4 tsp coarse ground pepper

Serving Info:

Yield: 1-1/4 cup
Servings: 5
Serving Size: 1/4 cup

RECIPE INFO

R D
0-1

- last checked 11/15/22 -
Use your mobile device's 'Camera' App to
look at this code for nutritional info.

Directions:

1. Add all of the ingredients into a bowl, whisk together till combined.
2. Let it rest, covered, for at least 2 hours, so the flavors can mellow.
3. Take a deep breath... and marvel in the fact I made a recipe with only 2 steps.

Notes:

- Scan the various jars of 'prepared horseradish' at the grocery store. Some have additives and are higher in points than others. Make sure to get a jar that's 0 points, period. 'Morehouse' brand prepared horseradish is 0 points for the entire jar.
- If you don't want to use white wine vinegar, lemon juice would also work well. If you can't eat lemons, go ahead and use regular distilled white vinegar. Honestly, it's only 1 tsp, it'll be fine.

Curry Cream Sauce

A Quick & Tasty Curry 'Base' Sauce, Perfect For Customizing

If you've ever wanted to try your hand at making a basic curry dish, but are too intimidated to get a bunch of exotic ingredients? This sauce is a simple and flavorful base you can toss together with things you most likely have in your pantry already. If you don't have curry powder already... you don't have to go looking for exotic blends. Start out simple and just get one from your local grocery store. No need to take a trip down the Silk Road.

Ingredients:

- 2 cups diced onion
- 3 medium garlic cloves, crushed, minced
- 2-1/2 tsp curry powder
- 3/4 tsp ground turmeric
- 2 cups fat free chicken broth
- 1/2 cup plain unsweetened almond milk (not Vanilla!!!!)
- 1-1/2 Tbsp cornstarch, dissolved into 2 Tbsp water
- cooking spray
- additional salt and pepper, to taste

Serving Info.:

Yields: 3-1/2 cups
Servings: 7
Serving Size: 1/2 cup

R D
0-0

- last checked 11/15/22 -
Use your mobile device's 'Camera' App to look at this code for nutritional info.

Directions:

1. Heat a medium sized pot over medium heat. Spray with cooking spray, then add the onions, curry powder and turmeric. Spray again with cooking spray, then cook over medium heat for 4-5 minutes, till onions begin to soften.
2. While the onions are cooking, occasionally use a wooden spoon to scrape the powders from the bottom of the pan, where they will start to collect and harden. You do not want to let them burn.
3. Add the garlic and cook for 2 more minutes.
4. Add the chicken broth, almond milk and dissolved cornstarch. Bring to a boil, reduce heat to medium, then cook at a boil for 5-6 minutes, till sauce begins to thicken.
5. Season with additional salt and pepper if desired.

Notes:

- THIS IS A BASE SAUCE! Customize it to however you want it. Feel free to add some lime juice, a little coconut milk, whatever you want. As is, this is a delicious, mild, non spicy base sauce.
- Add cooked protein into this sauce and let it simmer for a hearty 'curry' dish. Want to up it a bit? Add some potatoes and peas. Boom... quick, easy and simply curry.
- If you're allergic to almond milk, feel free to use ANY low calorie, milk-type beverage you can have, but adjust your points accordingly, if necessary.

Florentine Sauce

A delicously savory cream sauce loaded with fresh spinach

A Florentine Sauce is a savory cream sauce, loaded with fresh spinach, that is typically made with enough heavy cream and butter to give a T1000 a heart attack. This version is based on my Bechamel sauce. That's primarily because it's a great flavorful creamy base... aaaaaand because I'm lazy, so there's that.

Servings:

Yields: 4 cups
Servings: 8
Serving Size: 1/2 cup

R D
1-1

- last checked 11/15/22 -
Use your mobile device's 'Camera' App to
look at this code for nutritional info.

Ingredients:

- 1 prepared batch of my Bechamel sauce, recipe pg. 62, set aside.

- 3 medium garlic cloves, chopped
- 1 small onion, diced
- 1/4 cup fat free chicken broth
- 1 Tbsp white wine
- 1 Tbsp white wine vinegar
- 1 Tbsp lemon juice

- 4 cups fresh spinach, packed
    (2) 12oz bags of spinach works.
- Butter flavored cooking spray

Directions:

1 Cook the onions and garlic with butter flavored cooking spray for 2-3 minutes on medium heat, until they begin to soften. Add the broth, wine, vinegar and lemon juirce. Cook till most of the liquid has evaporated.
2 Rough chop the spinach, then add it to the pan. Cover and cook until just starting to wilt.
3 Pour in the prepared Bechamel sauce, stir to combine, then cover pan with lid and bring to a simmer. Cook at a low boil for 3-4 minutes.
4 Season with salt and pepper to taste

Notes:

- You can use frozen spinach if it is more convenient for you. Microwave it, then squeeze out all the liquid.
- You can replace the water and chicken bouillon with 1/4 cup of chicken broth and the sauce will stay 1 point per serving.
- Eating excessive amounts of spinach will **NOT** give you arms like Popeye.
- You can also ladle the sauce onto poached or scrambled eggs, atop an english muffin. It's a snazzy breakfast alternative to Eggs Benedict called Eggs Florentine.

Cook onions, garlic and spinach

Simmer with Bechamel

Use with Chicken, Seafood, and more

It's all Gravy Baby

This is honestly so simple that you're going to facepalm yourself

One of the most frequently requested sauces that I've been asked for that has always puzzled me, because honestly... it's really easy to make, is Gravy. Everyone always says that they miss gravy. I think it's because we're all so used to HAVING to make it 1 certain way, because "that's just how you make it." Get all of the fatty drippings from cooked meat, add a bunch of butter, or cream, or milk, with a garbage can full of flour used to thicken it. Why?!?! There's a really simple formula to make a low point gravy. Heat X amount of liquid, with Y amount of cornstarch, then you end up with Z amount of low point gravy. Its' easy and lower in points and calories.

Ingredients:

- 2 cups fat free chicken broth (see notes)
- 2 Tbsp PLUS 2 tsp cornstarch, stirred into the broth, till dissolved.
- 1/8 tsp black pepper
- salt to taste
- additional herbs or seasonings, as desired.

Directions:

1. Add all of the ingredients into a small sauce pot and stir till the cornstarch is dissolved completely.
2. Bring the mixture to a boil, over medium heat.
3. Reduce the heat and cook, uncovered, at a low boil for 4-5 minutes, or until the gravy begins to thicken to your desired consistency.
4. Remove from heat, season with additional salt and pepper, if desired. Pour into a dish and allow to cool for 5 minutes prior to serving. The gravy will continue to thicken slightly, as it cools.

Serving Info.:
Yields: 1-3/4 cups
Servings: 7
Serving Size: 1/4 cup

RECIPE INFO

R D
0-0

- last checked 11/15/22 -
Use your mobile device's 'Camera' App to look at this code for nutritional info.

Notes:

- You can easily double or triple this recipe to make a big ol' barrel of gravy and as long as you follow the formula for liquid to cornstarch ratio, it'll work just fine. However, adjust your points.
- You can use fat free beef broth, in place of my chicken broth, to make a beef gravy. However, it will add 1 ingredient point to the recipe.

Hollandaise Sauce

A luxuriously rich and creamy egg yolk and butter sauce

Hollandaise is pretty much the forbidden fruit of sauces when it comes to those of us trying to live a healthy lifestyle. Typically, we save up our points and calories to have the full fat version. The traditional sauce is a very thick, butter and egg yolk sauce, much like a warm mayonnaise. It's perfect over fish, vegetables and even potatoes. The most prized use for Hollandaise is, of course, Eggs Benedict, points be damned! Luckily for all of your waistlines, I've come up with a way to reduce the points for a good sized serving of the sauce, with some nifty ingredient swaps and... SCIENCE!

Ingredients:

- 1-1/2 cup water
- 3 Tbsp white wine vinegar *(or lemon juice)*
- 1 Tbsp white wine
- 1-1/2 tsp cornstarch
- 16 whole black peppercorns
- 2 bay leaves
- 2 Tbsp plus 1 tsp I Can't Believe It's Not Butter Light
- 6 second spray, butter flavored cooking spray ***
- 8 large egg yolks *(shout out to my good friend, Cholesterol!)*
- 1/8 tsp salt
- (optional) pinch of paprika or cayenne pepper, for garnish

Servings:

Yield: 1-1/2 cups
Servings: 6
Serving Size: 1/4 cup

RECIPE INFO

R D
1-1

- last checked 11/15/22 -
Use your mobile device's 'Camera' App to look at this code for nutritional info.

Directions:

1. In a small pot, stir together the water, wine, vinegar (or lemon juice), peppercorns, bay leaves and butter spread. Spray cooking spray into the pot, then bring to a rolling boil for 3 minutes. Turn off heat and set aside.
2. Allow mixture to cool for 20 minutes, then strain the liquid.
3. Return strained liquid to the pot, then stir in the cornstarch till dissolved. Whisk in the egg yolks and heat to a low simmer, stirring constantly as soon as the mixture begins to thicken.
4. Continue stirring on low heat, barely simmering for 5-7 minutes.
5. Turn off heat, season with additional salt, if needed.
6. Pour sauce through a strainer, to remove any cooked bits of egg. Pour strained sauce into a serving dish or spoon over food. Garnish with a pinch of either paprika or cayenne, if desired.

NOTES:

- Everyone has EXTREMELY picky opinion, when it comes to how they like their Hollandaise sauce. This recipe gives you a great low point sauce, so you can add your own tweaks.
- If you want a slightly more "yolk-like" color to your finished sauce, consider adding an 1/8 tsp dash of Turmeric. It will add a earthy hint, but will enhance the color, if that's a big deal to you. Remember, we're stretching 6 egg yolks to 1-1/2 cups.
- The sauce will thicken a little more as it cools due to the cornstarch. If it thickens too much, simply stir in water.
- If you want to be a little bit more Fancy Nancy, go ahead and add a little bit of fresh diced shallots to step 1.
- Yup... you're seeing that right. An entire 1/4 cup of Hollandaise sauce for just 1 point, Baby!!!

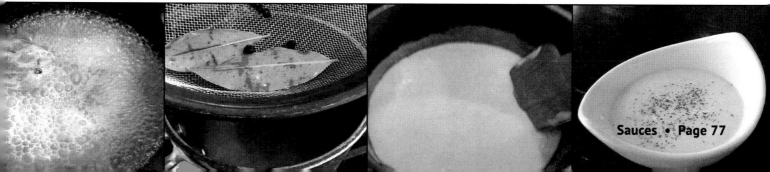

Katsu Sauce

My hacked down version of a deliciously savory, sweet and slightly spicy Japanese dipping sauce

Katsu sauce, or, Tonkatsu sauce, is a thick and savory sauce usually served with 'tonkatsu,' a breaded, deep fried Japanese pork cutlet. It is a thick worcestershire-based sauce which is usually VERY high in sugar, calories and points, due to its sugar. My recipe is a quick, skinnied-down version that is nooooot a traditional recipe. This is my hacked down version of Katsu sauce, which can be made in under 10 minutes.

Ingredients:

- 1/2 cup tomato sauce
- 3 Tbsp unsweetened applesauce
- 3 Tbsp PLUS 2 tsp worcestershire sauce
- 3 Tbsp low sodium soy sauce
- 2 Tbsp 'dark' soy sauce (optional, for color)
- 3 Tbsp rice vinegar
- 1/4 tsp onion powder
- 1/4 tsp black pepper
- 1 Tbsp 0 point sugar replacement o' choice
- 1-1/2 tsp cornstarch, dissolved into 2 tsp water

Serving Info:

Yield: 1 cup (and change)
Servings: 4
Serving Size: 1/4 cup

R D
1-1

- last checked 11/15/22 -
Use your mobile device's 'Camera' App to look at this code for nutritional info.

Directions:

1. Add all of the ingredients into a small pot, stir to combine.
2. Bring to a boil, reduce heat to medium, then cook at a rolling boil for 4-5 minutes, till thickened.
3. Remove from heat and let cool to room temperature, stirring every 10 minutes or so.

Notes:

- **DARK SOY SAUCE:** Dark soy sauce is NOT regular soy sauce, it IS called 'dark' soy sauce. If you want this dish to be a 10 out of 10, you need it, even if you have to buy it online. BE ADVISED!!!!! Different brands are different points. I use 'sushi chef' or 'Ka Me' brands.
- There are variations of Katsu sauce that are made with different fruits added in, mainly, prune and dates. If you'd like to add a slight fruity depth to your sauce, feel free to replace some of the tomato sauce with pureed fruit. Pureed fruit is 0 points if used in a sauce (unlike the smoothie-rule), because it's part of a dish which will be eaten as food, rather than drinking it. Don't you just love those loopholes.
- Well... some fruits, whole of blended, DO have points now if you're on the Diabetic plan.
- If you DO go the 'pureed fruit' route, to get more depth of flavor, blend up a couple of dates and prunes, then add them to the sauce. Along with tasting great, you'll get extra steps in, from running to the bathroom. Prunes... they're a giver.

Korean 'Gochujang' Sauce

If you enjoy Asian food, this sauce will knock your socks off. Even though it's' spicy, it's my hands-down favorite

Korean Gochujang sauce is fantastic. Prior to making it for the first time, while making my Asian cookbook (#5), I'd never had it before. It is one of my 3 favorite sauces in the world now. It DOES require a very exotic ingredient (for most of us), 'fermented red pepper paste', but it can be found in the Asian food aisle of most major grocery stores. This sauce is savory, slightly sweet, slightly fruity, spicy, a little sour. It's awesome.

Ingredients:

- 10 Tbsp (1/2 cup PLUS 2 Tbsp) Water
- 1-1/2 tsp cornstarch, dissolved into the water
- 3 Tbsp low sodium soy sauce
- 2 Tbsp 'dark' soy sauce (optional, for color)
- 3 Tbsp rice vinegar
- 1-1/2 Tbsp sugar free syrup (pancake)
- 2-1/2 Tbsp no sugar added ketchup, or tomato sauce
- 2 tsp sugar free strawberry preserves/jelly
- 4 Tbsp fermented red pepper paste (gochujang paste)
- 1/4 tsp sesame oil
- 2 medium garlic cloves, crushed, minced
- 1/2 Tbsp ginger, minced
- 6 Tbsp 0 point sugar replacement o' choice
- 1/2 tsp salt

Serving Info:

Yield: 1-1/2 cup
Servings: 6
Serving Size: 1/4 cup

RECIPE INFO   R D
1-1

- last checked 11/15/22 -
Use your mobile device's 'Camera' App to
look at this code for nutritional info.

Directions:

1. Add all of the ingredients together in a small pot. Stir till well combined, then bring to a boil over medium heat.
2. Cook at a low boil for 5-6 minutes, or until the sauce begins to thicken.
3. Remove from heat, set aside to cool. Stirring occasionally while it cools.

Notes:

- **ASIAN RED PEPPER PASTE:** Can be found in the Asian Food aisle of most major chain grocery stores. Do a google image search to see what it looks like. It might also be found as 'Gochujang' red pepper paste. Different brands of fermented red pepper paste have varying point values. The brand I used was only 4 points for 1/4 cup, others are 5 points. The points of your dish may vary, based on the brand you use.
- **DARK SOY SAUCE:** Dark soy sauce is NOT regular soy sauce, it IS called 'dark' soy sauce. If you want this dish to be a 10 out of 10, you need it, even if you have to buy it online. BE ADVISED!!!!! Different brands are different points. I use 'sushi chef' or 'Ka Me' brands.

10 Minute Marinara

Let me start off by pointing out the elephant in the room. I KNOW that there are going to be a lot of you that think that you can NOT have an amazing Marinara sauce, without using fancy ingredients, slow simmering a pot o' tomato sauce for 8 hours, all while listening to The Godfather soundtrack. Well, I'm not a Sicilian Grandma with 4 knees, I'm a busy dad with 2 kids and no time. In the past year I've had to streamline my original sauce and come up with a version that can be thrown together, fast... because, well... kids. Ya'know what? It's actually really danged good. It comes together extremely fast, yet is extremely flavorful and is a great base to build off of.

Ingredients:

- 4-6 second spray, olive oil cooking spray
- 1/4 tsp olive oil
- 4 medium garlic cloves
- 1 small onion, diced
- 1/2 cup chicken broth
- 1 tsp dried basil
- 1 tsp dried oregano
- 1 tsp dried parsley
- 1 Tbsp red wine
- 1 Tbsp red wine vinegar
- 1 to 2 tsp 0 point sweetener o' choice
- 45oz canned tomato sauce (a 15 and a 30 oz can)
- 1/2 tsp salt
- 1/4 tsp pepper

Yield: 5 cups
Servings: 10
Serving Size: 1/2 cup

R   D
0-0

- last checked 11/15/22 -
Use your mobile device's 'Camera' App to
look at this code for nutritional info.

Directions:

1. Dice the onion and set aside. Chop the garlic and set aside. Put a medium sized pot on your stove and turn the heat up to a medium-high flame, then, get to work. *whip crack*
2. After the pot has had a minute to get nice and hot... add the olive oil and cooking spray. Immediately add the onions and cook for 2-3 minutes, until they start to sweat, then add the garlic, chicken broth, wine, vinegar, dried herbs and sweetener. It will begin bubbling immediately. Allow to cook for 1-2 minutes, or until most of the liquid has dissolved.
3. Pour in the tomato sauce, add the salt and pepper, then bring to a low boil. Pour the sauce into a food processor or blender, or you can use an immersion blender to puree the sauce. Process until the onions are broken down and the sauce is smooth.
4. Season with additional salt and pepper if desired. Done.

Notes:

- You can use sugar instead of artifical sweetener, but you'll need to adjust points accordingly.
- This sauce has no points whatsoever. Feel free to customize it. Add some more olive oil, an extra bit of wine, some additional fresh herbs... whatever you want. This sauce is FAST, GOOD, and perfect for using as a base for your own sauce.
- Feel free to get food-snobby and say you haaaaaave to slow simmer marinara for 8 hours, using imported San Marzano tomatoes and 12 year old balsamic. While you're doing that, I'll be over here changing diapers and doing the dishes. 😉 🤣

Marsala Wine Sauce

Is It Possible To Have A Healthy Marsala Sauce? Why, Yes... Yes It Is.

This is my healthy, fat free take on a traditional Marsala wine sauce, used most commonly for Chicken Marsala. It's loaded with diced onions, sliced mushrooms, garlic, beef broth and 2 different wines. This is honestly the first time in my life I've ever had Chicken Marsala... and I thought it was really tasty.

Ingredients:

- 1 medium onion, diced
- 3-4 garlic cloves, crushed/chopped
- 16 oz sliced mushrooms, any variety. I bought 2 of the standard sized 8oz packages, in the produce department.
- 1-1/2 cups fat free beef broth
- 6-1/2 Tbsp marsala wine (dry, or sweet, doesn't matter)
- 1 Tbsp 'red wine', any type. I'm not a wine snob.
- 1/2 tsp salt
- 1/4 tsp pepper
- 2-1/2 Tbsp cornstarch, dissolved into 3 Tbsp water
- Fresh chopped parsley, for garnish (optional)

Serving Info.:

Yields: 4 cups
Servings: 5
Serving Size: 3/4 cup

RECIPE INFO

R D
1-1

- last checked 11/15/22 -
Use your mobile device's 'Camera' App to look at this code for nutritional info.

Directions:

1. Heat a LARGE pan over medium-high heat for 1 minute. Spray with cooking spray, then add the onion, garlic and mushrooms. Spray with a little more cooking spray, then cook for 5 minutes, or until they begin to soften and darken in color. (from pic. 1 to pic 2)
2. Add the beef broth, marsala wine and red wine to the pan. Then pour in the dissolved cornstarch. Stir till the cornstarch is thoroughly mixed into the sauce. Add salt and pepper.
3. Bring to a simmer, then reduce heat to medium and cook at a boil for 5-6 minutes, or until the sauce thickens nicely.
4. If desired, garnish with fresh chopped parsley, season with additional salt/pepper if needed.

Notes:

- 2 Wines??: Roll with it... it's a 'Points' thing.
- "Can I halve the recipe, Daniel?" .... Yeah... You can halve ANY recipe.
- Does it matter if I get 'sweet' Marsala wine, or 'dry' Marsala wine? Personal preference. I had to google it. I used 'dry' in my recipe and I really enjoyed the flavor.
- But Daniel... I don't drink alcohol... what can I use instead of the wine... for this wine sauce? I'd swap both wines out for 1/4 cup water and 1/4 cup fat free chicken broth and 1/4 cup red wine vinegar. It won't taste the same, but it'll still be good. If you're wondering why not add more beef broth... because any more than 1-1/2 cups of fat free beef broth gains 1 point.

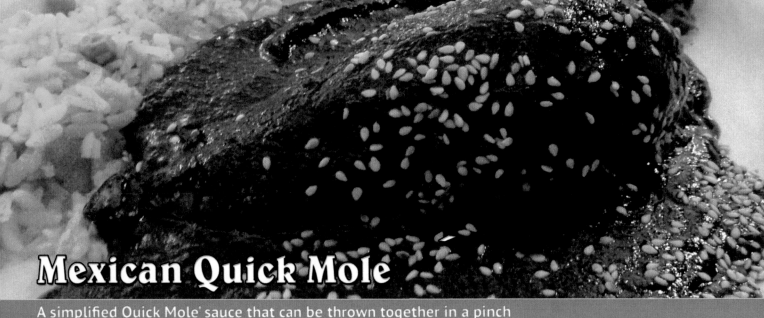

Mexican Quick Mole

A simplified Quick Mole' sauce that can be thrown together in a pinch

Get ready to dodge angry mobs wielding torches and pitchforks because we're about to tackle the most holy of Mexican sauces, Mole' Poblano. Traditionally, Mole' is a very labor intensive sauce that takes an extremely long time to make and includes ingredients like bread, toasted nuts, seeds, peppers, oil, plantains and much more. It usually cooks for hours or even days. This one is ultra fast, flavorful and only 1 point for a 1/2 cup serving.

Serving Size:

Yields: 6 cups
Servings: 12
Serving Size: 1/2 cup servings

- *last checked 11/15/22 -*
Use your mobile device's 'Camera' App to look at this code for nutritional info.

Ingredients:

- 3-4 medium garlic cloves, chopped
- 29 oz canned tomato sauce
- 1/4 cup 0 point sweetener of choice (monkfruit, stevia, swerve, etc.)
- 3 Tbsp PLUS 2 tsp unsweetened cocoa powder
- 1/4 tsp black pepper
- 1 to 2 tsp chili powder, OR chipotle chili powder. Season to spice preference.
- 1-1/2 tsp ground cumin
- 1 tsp ground cinnamon
- 2 cups fat free chicken broth
- 2 Tbsp PB2 or other brand powdered peanut butter
- 2 Tbsp masa harina (instant masa mix, or any brand corn flour... not cornmeal!)
- 1 tsp onion powder
- 2 Tbsp Lily's 'stevia sweetened' mini dark chocolate, or semi sweet chocolate chips
- 3 tsp sesame seeds, for toasting
- 1/4 tsp sesame oil (optional, adding it to the sauce, gives a subtle, nutty flavor)

Directions:

1. Spray a medium sized pot with cooking spray and cook the garlic till just fragrant.
2. Add the tomato sauce, sweetener, cocoa powder, black pepper, chili powder, cumin, cinnamon,broth, powdered peanut butter, masa harina, onion powder, chocolate chips and sesame oil to the pot. Bring to a boil, then lower the heat, cover and simmer for 15-20 mins.
3. Turn off heat and let cool for 30 minutes.
4. Toast the sesame seeds in a small pan over medium heat for 3-4 minutes, till starting to brown, set aside to use as a garnish on your plated meal.

Note:
- Toasting the sesame seeds adds an extra step, but it really gives them a much more pronounced flavor.
- 'Instant Masa Mix' can be found in the Mexican food aisle, at your grocery store. It is usually sold under the brand name 'Ma Se Ca' or 'Maseca' instant tamale mix.

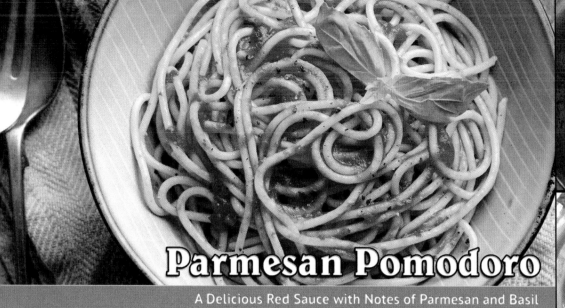

Parmesan Pomodoro

A Delicious Red Sauce with Notes of Parmesan and Basil

This is an extremly simply sauce, with tremendous depth of flavor. The traditional version calls for San Marzano tomatoes, though you are more than welcome to use regular canned tomato sauce. I won't judge. Also, I'd like to apologize to all of my Italian Nona's that follow me. Don't take my use of Kraft cheese sprinkle's TOO personally... I have kids. lol

Ingredients:

- 1 tsp olive oil
- olive oil cooking spray
- 1/2 cup onions, diced
- 4 medium garlic cloves, crushed and chopped
- (2) 30 oz cans of either whole, peeled, 'San Marzano' tomatoes... or you can use normal canned tomato sauce, if you don't want to be fancy.
- 1/4 cup fresh basil, chopped, packed
- 2 Tbsp PLUS 2-3/4 tsp reduced fat Parmesan topping (like Kraft... see notes)
- 1/4 tsp salt
- 1/4 tsp pepper

Serving Info.:

Yields: 6 cups
Servings: 12
Serving Size: 1/2 cup

R   D
0-0

- last checked 11/15/22 -
Use your mobile device's 'Camera' App to look at this code for nutritional info.

Directions:

1. Heat a medium sized pot for 1 minute. Add the olive oil, onions and garlic. Spray with additional olive oil cooking spray and cook till onions begin to soften, 4-5 minutes.
2. Add the onions into a food processor or blender, with the canned tomatoes. Process till smooth.
3. Add the fresh chopped basil into the food processor (or blender) and blend till smooth.
4. Return sauce to the pot, stir in the Parmesan, then simmer for 15 minutes. Season with salt and pepper. Done.

Notes:

- PARMESAN: If you are a purist and do NOT want to use Kraft reduced fat parmesan grated topping... Use any type of parmesan you want. MY recipe's points account for 3 points of cheese. If you'd like to use the regular stuff, adjust your recipe.
- CANNED TOMATOES: I wanted to use actual 'San Marzano' tomatoes for my sauce. My local store only sells canned WHOLE San Marzano tomatoes, which is why my ingredients mention 'whole' tomatoes. If you just want to use good ol' fashioned regular tomatoes... don't buy canned whole tomatoes. Buy canned 'tomato sauce'. It's cheaper and will still taste great.
- Though this recipe is tasty, I have it on good authority that @chiafullo's favorite Pomodoro sauce is from The Olive Garden.

Pesto Sauce

A fresh, vibrant, savory & versatile green sauce

Pesto is an extremely delicious sauce, primarily consisting of finely processed garlic, tons of basil, different herbs and lots and lots and lots (did I say lots yet?) of olive oil. It is insanely yummy, but insanely high in points. Even popular "skinny" pesto recipes are typically a few points for a small 2 tablespoon serving size. We're upping our game by getting more olive oil flavor with some olive oil cooking spray, minimizing the amount of actual oil, then stretching it with warm water.

Ingredients:

- 1 Tbsp pine nuts, toasted
- 3-4 medium garlic cloves
- 3 cups basil, stems ok, chopped ***
- 3 cups spinach, packed, chopped ***
- 1/4 cup reduced fat grated parmesan topping (like Kraft brand)
- 1 cup warm water
- 2 tsp lemon juice
- 1 Tbsp olive oil (get a bottle that says Robust, Bold, or some other word that denotes a 'strong' flavor.)
- 1/2 tsp salt
- 1/4 tsp fresh ground pepper
- olive oil cooking spray, 6-8 second spray ***

Directions:

1 Heat a small sauce pan over medium-low heat for 1 minute, then add the pine nuts. Warm the pine nuts for 2-3 minutes, moving them around the pan, till toasted. Set aside.
2 Place all of the ingredients, including the pine nuts, into a food processor or large blender. Spray the olive oil cooking spray for 5 seconds directly onto the ingredients at close range to give them a fair amount of 0 point olive oil flavoring.
3 Process the mixture to break down all of the basil and spinach. Season with additional salt and pepper if desired.

NOTE:

- Basil can be expensive and some folks can't have Spinach, due to dietary restrictions. There are TONS of different greens you can use instead. Experiment with watercress, arugala, kale, collards, mustard greens, even peas. Look online for basil-free Pesto recipes for ideas.
- You can also sub. chopped walnuts in place of the pine nuts. Those babies are expensive too.

Servings:

Yields: 2 cups
Servings: 8
Serving Size: 1/4 cup

- last checked 11/15/22 -
Use your mobile device's 'Camera' App to
look at this code for nutritional info.

Piccata Sauce

Garlic, Lemon and Salty, Briny, Capery Awesomeness

In full disclosure, I understand that most of you reading this are thinking "What the heck is a caper?!" Yes, it COULD be a sneaky plan or bank heist, but it's also a tiny little ball of briny, salty goodness that looks kind of like a tiny sweet pea. I STRONGLY recommend that you buy and cook with *"Non Pareille"* capers. It's written on the jars, it just means those are small capers. Don't use the larger capers, as those are just a big salty jar full of yuck. You can find capers in the grocery store by the olives and vinegars typically.

Ingredients:

- 2-3 garlic cloves, chopped
- 6-8 second spray, butter flavored cooking spray
- 1-1/2 cups fat free chicken broth
- 2-1/2 Tbsp lemon juice
- 1 Tbsp cornstarch, dissolved in 1 Tbsp water
- 1/4 tsp olive oil (use a bottle that says 'robust' or 'bold')
- 1 Tbsp I Can't Believe It's Not Butter Light**
- 2 Tbsp capers
- 1 tsp dried parsley flakes
- Salt and pepper to taste
- Thin lemon slices for garnish
- Fresh chopped parsley for garnish

Serving Info.:

Yields: 1-1/2 cups
Servings: 3
Serving Size: 1/2 cup

RECIPE INFO R D
[1-1]

- last checked 11/15/22 -
Use your mobile device's 'Camera' App to
look at this code for nutritional info.

Directions:

1 Sweat the garlic in a medium pan with cooking spray, until it becomes fragrant. Add the broth, lemon juice, olive oil and butter spread. Stir to combine, heat to a rolling boil.
2 Stir in the capers, parsley flakes dissolved cornstarch. Return to a simmer, stirring frequently.
3 Once the sauce begins to thicken, add a few thin lemon slices and stir around in the sauce.
4 It should take around 1 minute for the lemons to begin to soften and break down. Turn off the heat, season with salt and pepper to taste, then spoon the finished sauce over your meat.

Note:

- For best results, add your cooked meat to the pan and allow to simmer in the sauce for a minute, turning to coat.
- As with everything I make, this sauce is tasty as-is, however it's so low in points and calories that you have plenty of room to add some more butter spread or olive oil.

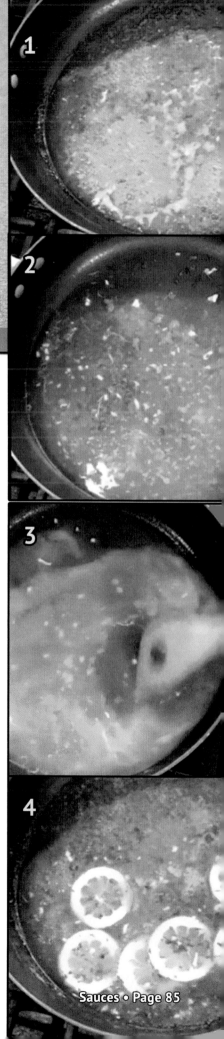

Pineapple Chili Sauce & Marinade

This sweet and refreshing sauce has an herby, slightly spicy kick from crushed red pepper flakes

This is an incredibly simple sauce to make, which also works as a fantastic marinade for meats. The vibrant sweetness of the pineapple, with the tart lime juice, hint of garlic and the pop of cilantro, along with the slight pepperiness, make this a very simple yet complex sauce. It tastes better the longer it rests, prior to use.

Ingredients:

- 3 cups pineapple chunks (fresh)
- 1/4 cup cilantro, chopped & loosely packed
- 1 small garlic clove, around 1/2 tsp minced
- 1 Tbsp lime juice
- 1/2 tsp crushed red pepper flakes
- pinch of salt, to taste
- Patience

Serving Info:

Yield: 2-1/4 cups
Servings: 9
Serving Size: 1/4 cup

R D
0-1

- last checked 11/15/22 -
Use your mobile device's 'Camera' App to
look at this code for nutritional info.

Directions:

1. Place all of the ingredinets into a blender or food processor.
2. Process until smooth, then place into a bowl and allow to rest, in the fridge, for at least 1 hour. The longer it rests, the more the flavors develop. Trust me.

Notes:

- Though I highly, highly recommend using fresh pineapple, you CAN use canned, rinsed/drained pineapple chunks, in a pinch. It won't taste AS great as a sauce, but will work fine as a marinade. It will also be a thinner, more watery mixture if using canned pineapple.
- I'm not lying when I say it tastes better the longer it sits. When I first made this sauce I tried some immediately... it tasted ok. I set it in the fridge and tried it again an hour later, it had a much better flavor. After 2-3 hours it was fantastic. This is a great make-ahead sauce.
- The acidity of this sauce makes it a great marinade for not just imparting flavor, but also tenderizing whatever you marinate in it.
- This sauce gains points for folks on the Diabetic plan, due to the pineapple.

Red Enchilada Sauce

This is a very fast, low fat and simple take on a Mexican classic

I need to start by addressing all of my Latino amigos that are reading this page. I understand that I've already messed with your Mole' sauce, I've already had you put fat free yogurt into Masa to make 3 point Gringo Tamales on Connect (#dhallakvids), I know that right now you're probably waving your fists in the sky and yelling "what more could this guy do to us?!" Well sorry, but I'm messing with your enchilada sauce now. Traditionally, red enchilada sauce is an incredibly delicious and spicy (depending on the peppers you use) puree of water, seasonings, a BOAT LOAD of oil and tons and tons and tons of dried hot chili peppers. In order to make it really low in points, we need to eliminate the oil. That's why I decided to replace it with tomato sauce and regular chili powder from the spice aisle. The reason being that it is more readily available to people and the thought of dealing with a big bag of dried chili peppers is an intimidating turn off to a lot of folks.

Ingredients:

- 2 cups fat free chicken broth
- 1/2 cup water
- 1 to 2 tsp chili powder, to taste. You can use regular chili powder, or other varieties, such as chipotle and anaheim chili powders, or a combination of them.
- 1/8 to 1/4 tsp cayenne pepper, **(OPTIONAL!).** Only use the cayenne if you want to make it a spicier enchilada sauce. It's fine without it.
- 1-1/2 tsp garlic powder
- 1-1/2 tsp onion powder
- 1-1/2 tsp ground cumin
- 1/4 to 1/2 tsp salt, to taste
- 30 oz canned tomato sauce

Directions:

1 Pour ALL of the ingredients into a medium sized pot and stir to combine over medium heat.
2 Bring the sauce to a boil, then cover and reduce the heat to a low simmer. Allow sauce to simmer covered for 15 minutes, stirring occasionally.
3 Remove from heat and season to taste.

Serving Size:

Yields: 6 cups
Servings: 12
Serving Size: 1/2 cup

R D
0-0

- last checked 11/15/22 -
*Use your mobile device's 'Camera' App to
look at this code for nutritional info.*

NOTES:

- Various types of dried chili powders can be found in the spice aisle (McCormick's sells chipotle chili powder), or usually in the Latin section of most supermarkets.
- Different brands of chili powder have different levels of heat. Adjust your spice used. Start small, add more to taste.
- Pairing this sauce with 1 point tortillas or wraps, shredded chicken, veggies, and the Fat Free cheese hack will give you some extreeemely legit, low point enchiladas.
- This sauce goes really well with my low point Tamales. You can find them in on my website in the 'featured recipes' section, as well as in my YouTube channel. You can also search in Connect for *#dhallaktamales*. If you scroll down, you'll find a video of me making them.

Roasted Red Pepper Marinara

A mildly sweet marinara-style sauce made with roasted red peppers

A couple years ago, a good friend from Connect, asked if I could make a marinara sauce with something other than tomatoes. After a little searching online, I found that making marinara sauce with Roasted Red Peppers is a great way to do it. The addition of red wine, chicken broth and the sauteed carrots and red onion also help give it more depth of flavor.

Ingredients:

- 5 large red bell peppers, chopped
- 5 medium cloves fresh garlic
- olive oil cooking spray ***
- 1 large red onion, rough chopped
- 1-1/2 cups chopped carrots
- 1-1/4 tsp italian seasoning
- 1/2 tsp garlic powder
- 1/2 tsp onion powder
- 1/2 tsp dried basil
- 1/2 tsp dried thyme
- 1 Tbsp I Can't Believe It's Not Butter Light
- 2 cups fat free chicken broth
- 3 Tbsp red wine
- 5-1/2 tsp (1 Tbsp PLUS 2-1/2 tsp) balsamic vinegar

Serving Info.:

Yields: 5 cups
Serving Size: 1/2 cup
Servings: 10

RECIPE INFO

R   D
0-0

- last checked 11/15/22 -
Use your mobile device's 'Camera' App to
look at this code for nutritional info.

Directions:

1. Preheat your oven to 425 degrees and line a sheet pan with aluminum foil,
2. Cut the red peppers into large pieces, remove the seeds and arrange on the sheet pan along with the fresh cloves of garlic. Coat with olive oil cooking spray, make sure it's a 0 point amount of spray. Season lightly with salt and pepper, then bake at 425 for 20-25 minutes. Remove when the peppers are cooked through and pliable.
3. Spray a large saucepan with cooking spray and saute' the red onion and carrots for 2-3 minutes on medium-high heat. Add the butter spread and stir till it melts. Add the italian seasoning, garlic powder, onion powder, dried basil, thyme, balsamic vinegar and wine. Bring to a boil and allow to simmer for 3-4 minutes.
4. Pour the contents of the sauce pan into a food processor or large blender, along with all of the roasted garlic and red bell peppers. Peeling the skins from the peppers is optional.
5. Puree on high speed for a minimum of 1 minute or until the sauce is smooth, adding more broth, if desired, to thin the sauce more. Season with salt and pepper, to taste.

Note:

- If you don't want to use red wine in your sauce, you can remove it. Increase your red wine vinegar to 3 Tbsp, instead.
- If you're allergic to tomatoes, but can have bell peppers... use this as a tomato sauce replacement in recipes, but adjust seasonings.
- If you want to take the time to do it... peel the skins off of the roasted peppers. I'm lazy.

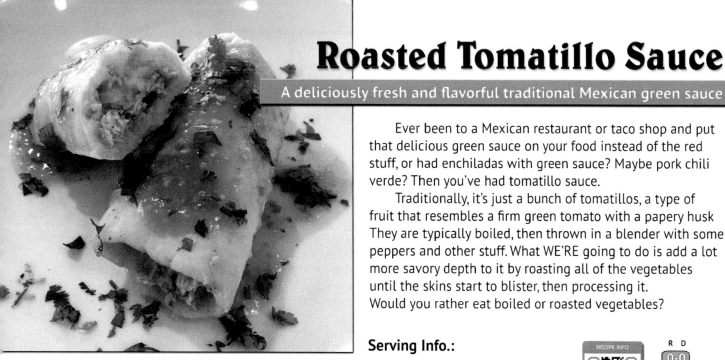

Roasted Tomatillo Sauce

A deliciously fresh and flavorful traditional Mexican green sauce

Low point chicken tamales with roasted tomatillo sauce

Ever been to a Mexican restaurant or taco shop and put that delicious green sauce on your food instead of the red stuff, or had enchiladas with green sauce? Maybe pork chili verde? Then you've had tomatillo sauce.

Traditionally, it's just a bunch of tomatillos, a type of fruit that resembles a firm green tomato with a papery husk They are typically boiled, then thrown in a blender with some peppers and other stuff. What WE'RE going to do is add a lot more savory depth to it by roasting all of the vegetables until the skins start to blister, then processing it.
Would you rather eat boiled or roasted vegetables?

Serving Info.:
Yield: 5 cups
Servings: 10 servings
Serving Size: 1/2 cup

RECIPE INFO

R D
0-0

- last checked 11/15/22 -
Use your mobile device's 'Camera' App to look at this code for nutritional info.

Ingredients:

- 2-1/2 lbs. Tomatillos, husks and stems removed
- 1 medium onion, rough chopped
- 2 medium green bell peppers, rough chopped, seeds removed
- 3 medium garlic cloves
- 4 good sized Poblano peppers, chopped, seeds removed (they aren't spicy)
- 1/2 bunch fresh cilantro, around 1 handful
- 1/2 tsp salt
- 1 whole Jalapeno pepper *(OPTIONAL!)*

Directions:

1. Preheat your oven to 375 degrees.
2. Line a large sheet pan with foil and spray with olive oil cooking spray.
3. Place all of the vegetables on the tray and spray them liberally with the cooking spray, then sprinkle lightly with salt and pepper.
4. Cook the vegetables at 375 degrees for 45 minutes, or until the tops of the vegetables are starting to blacken.
5. Turn the broiler to high in your oven and place the tray on the top rack under the broiler. Watch so that the vegetables don't burn to a crisp. You want to develop some black char across the tops of some of them.
6. Remove the tray from the oven and spoon all of the roasted veggies into a food processor or large blender. Make sure to also pour all of the juices in as well, along with the fresh cilantro and 1/4 tsp salt.
7. Process the vegetables on high for up to 1 minute. It should give you a thick green salsa.

Notes:

- Tomatillos are very easy to clean for this sauce, just pull the husks back like the husks on an ear of corn, twist the stem and pull. Remove any dirt or debris and you're good to go.
- Tomatillos have a sticky feel to them, that's fine.
- Add the Jalapeno to the roasting pan, if you want a spicy sauce. This base recipe is for a completely mild and non spicy sauce.
- If you plan to use this sauce for enchiladas, add some water or chicken broth to thin it out a bit.
- This sauce is delicious served with tacos, tamales, over chicken, pork, on nachos, enchiladas, eggs, pretty much anything.

Scampi Sauce

A spicy, lemon butter, white wine, garlic, herb sauce

Scampi sauce is a delicious, zesty, herbed lemon garlic sauce that goes fantastic with all types of seafood and poultry. It's most popular application is, of course, Shrimp Scampi. In this recipe I'll be adding Shrimp into the ingredients, even though this is really supposed to be a recipe page for just the sauce. I'm including how to actually use it to make a dish,.. why not, it's my book after all.

Ingredients:

- 4 medium garlic cloves, chopped
- 5 second spray, butter flavored cooking spray ***
- 1-1/2 cup fat free chicken broth
- 3 Tbsp white wine
- 2 Tbsp white wine vinegar
- 1 Tbsp PLUS 1-1/2 tsp cornstarch, dissolved in 2 Tbsp water
- 1 Tbsp I can't believe it's not butter Light
- 2 Tbsp lemon juice
- 1/4 tsp salt
- 1/8 tsp black pepper
- 1/8 - 1/4 tsp red pepper flakes to taste
- 1 Tbsp fresh parsley, finely chopped
- 2 Tbsp fresh oregano, finely chopped

Servings:

Yields: 1-3/4 cup sauce
Servings: 3 (and change)
Servin Size: 1/2 cup sauce

RECIPE INFO
R D
1-1

- last checked 11/15/22 -
Use your mobile device's 'Camera' App to look at this code for nutritional info.

Directions:

1. Spray a medium saucepan for 5 seconds with olive oil cooking spray, then saute garlic over medium heat till fragrant.

2. Add the broth, wine, vinegar, dissolved cornstarch, butter spread, lemon juice, salt, and pepper to the pan. Bring to a rolling boil for 3 minutes, allowing the sauce to start thickening.

3. Add red pepper flakes, parsley and oregano to the pan, continue cooking at a low simmer for an additional 2 minutes, or until the sauce coats the back of a spoon. Done.

4. Additionally, if you want to make a traditional shrimp or chicken scampi dish, now would be the time when you'd add your raw shrimp or diced raw chicken to the simmering sauce. If cooking shrimp, place the shrimp into the simmering scampi sauce and toss to coat. Cook for 2 minutes or until the shrimp is a light pink color throughout. Cook chicken slightly longer, till cooked through.

A2 Steak Sauce

A Complex, Yet Simple To Make Steak Sauce Using Pantry Staples (minus 1 ingredient... c'mon, folks... I try!)

First off... no, this isn't an A1 steak sauce copycat... I just like humor. So, rather than trying to make a copycat recipe which nobody would be happy about, because I tried multiple ones and none of them tasted right... I tried making my own recipe, from scratch. The tricky part was in order to keep the points down to 1 point for a 1/4 cup serving, I had to stretch the balsamic and worcestershire with white vinegar.

Ingredients:

- 1/2 cup water with 1-1/2 tsp cornstarch stirred into it.
- 4-1/2 Tbsp balsamic vinegar
- 3-1/2 Tbsp worcestershire sauce
- 3 Tbsp white vinegar
- 1 Tbsp lemon juice
- 1/2 tsp asian 'fish' sauce (weird, but worth it)
- 1/3 cup tomato sauce
- 1 Tbsp dijon mustard
- 2 tsp 0 point brown sugar replacement
- 1/4 tsp molasses
- 3/4 to 1 tsp salt, to taste(sounds like a lot, but trust me, Susie!)
- 3/4 tsp onion powder
- 1/2 tsp garlic powder
- 1/2 tsp cracked black pepper (or coarse ground)
- 2 tsp whole black peppercorns
- 1/8 tsp hot sauce, any brand you prefer

Serving Info:

Yield: 1 cup
Servings: 4
Serving Size: 1/4 cup

R D
1-1

RECIPE INFO

- last checked 11/15/22 -
Use your mobile device's 'Camera' App to look at this code for nutritional info.

Directions:

1. Dissolve the cornstarch with the water, then heat ALL of the ingredients in a small pot, over medium-high heat, till boiling.
2. Reduce heat, cook at a medium boil for 6 minutes, stirring occasionally.
3. Remove sauce from heat, pour through a fine wire strainer, into a bowl. Let cool to room temperature. While cooling, stir the sauce every now and then, to ensure the cooling cornstarch doesn't create a thin layer on the top. The flavor develops more depth, the longer you let it sit.

Notes:

- FISH SAUCE!?!: Yup, in the asian food aisle. One of the reasons worcestershire sauce has such a nice, savory depth, is because it has anchovy in it. However, we can't add anymore worcesterwhire sauce, or it goes up in points. What can we add in its place? A dash of Asian 'fish' sauce. It gives Thai dishes a tremendous flavor punch, because it contains... you guessed it, anchovy.. If you're on the fence, it gets used a LOT in cookbook 5.
- SWEETENER: You can use regular sweetener, but the flavor will be a little different.

Teriyaki Sauce

My quick & tasty take on the traditional Japanese sauce/glaze. Did I mention... it's toootally non-traditional?

Everyone who's ever had cheap Asian fast food at a strip mall, KNOWS what Teriyaki chicken is, or rather... ya'll think you do. What you're really eating is sugar water with soy sauce. For my recipe, I took a traditional Japanese recipe, then used ingredient hacks to completely rebuild it. This version is quick, easy, is absolutely delicious and has a nice depth of flavor. It works great as sauce, glaze, or as a dip.

Ingredients:

- 3/4 cup water
- 1-1/2 tsp cornstarch
- 2 Tbsp 0 point sweetener o' choice PLUS 1/4 tsp molasses, *or*... 2 Tbsp 0 point brown sugar replacement
- 1-1/2 Tbsp sugar free syrup (pancake syrup)
- 3 Tbsp low sodium soy sauce
- 1 medium garlic clove, minced
- 1 tsp ginger, minced
- 1/8 tsp salt
- pinch of red pepper flakes (optional)

Serving Info:

Yield: 1 cup
Servings: 4
Serving Size: 1/4 cup

RECIPE INFO   R   D
0-0

- last checked 11/15/22 -
Use your mobile device's 'Camera' App to
look at this code for nutritional info.

Directions:

1. Dissolve the cornstarch with the water, then heat ALL of the ingredients in a small pot, over medium-high heat, till boiling.
2. Reduce heat, cook at a low rolling boil for 4-5 minutes.
3. Remove sauce from heat, pour into a bowl and let cool to room temperature. Done

Notes:

- If you have access to 0 point brown sugar substitute, swap the 2 Tbsp of sweetener and 1/4 tsp of molasses, with 2 Tbsp of 0 point brown sugar substitute. It makes a huge difference. In your local grocery store or walmart you might find Truvia brand 0 calorie brown sugar replacement, Swerve brand, or Lakanto brand.
- If you'd like to use this a glaze, let it continue to simmer longer, so that it reduces to the consistency of syrup.

Tzatziki Sauce

The favorite sauce of Gus Portokalos, King of the Greeks. This delicious sauce is creamy, refreshing and brings a bright 'pop' to any dish, thanks to loads of minced cucumber, fresh dill, mint and lemon juice. It's commonly slathered on EVERYTHING Greek, including Gyro sandwiches. "You give me a sauce... aaaaany sauce... and I tell'a you how the root of'a that sauce... iz'a Greek."

Ingredients:

- 1 cup plain fat free Greek yogurt
- 1/2 cup cucumber. Peeled, finely chopped/minced and pressed between paper towels to remove excess liquid.
- 1 Tbsp lemon juice
- 1 tsp olive oil
- 1 small garlic clove, crushed, finely chopped
- 1 Tbsp fresh dill, finely chopped, loosely packed
- 1/2 tsp fresh mint, finely minced (optional)
- 1/4 tsp salt

Serving Info:

Yield: 1-1/4 cups
Servings: 5
Serving Size: 1/4 cup

R D
0-1

- last checked 11/15/22 -
Use your mobile device's 'Camera' App to look at this code for nutritional info.

Directions:

1. Peel 1/2 of a medium sized cucumber. Finely mince/dice it, then press the minced cucumber onto paper towels, to remove as much of the excess liquid as possible. Yes... I know I'm repeating this from the ingredients, but it's important. Set aside.
2. Finely mince the fresh dill and mint (if using), as well as the garlic clove, set aside.
3. Mix all of the ingredients together in a bowl, till well combined. Set aside in the fridge for at least 1 hour. The flavors will develop much more, if allowed to rest.

Notes:

- If you don't have access to fresh herbs, you can use dried dill and dried mint, however, the flavor won't be the same. IF you end up using dried herbs, I'd recommend 1-1/2 tsp dried dill and 1/4 tsp dried mint. You'll also definitely need to let the sauce rest, for the herbs to absorb some of the moisture from the yogurt.
- As mentioned above, the mint is optional.
- Don't have fresh garlic? Not a problem. Use 1/4 tsp garlic powder. It'll work in a pinch, though the flavor will obviously be a little different.
- Cucumber: If it'd make you sleep better at night, you can choose to remove the 'seeds' of your cucumber. I didn't, but you can. You do you, Boo.

Vodka Sauce

A Robust and Flavorful Tomato Sauce with an Adult Kick

This sauce was a direct result of a post that I saw trending in Connect, from member **@libra.1019**, saying how much she missed pasta with Vodka sauce, and that the advice she received at her workshop was more focused on "eat the regular full fat version, but a smaller portion, this is a lifestyle", which I call BS on. Why have a small, unsatisfying fatty micro meal, when you can have a healthy, regular sized version that's lower in calories, fat and points than the sad little tiny plate? So... here we are. This Vodka sauce is a modern take on a classic tomato sauce. Infused with lots sauteed onions, garlic, fresh basil, black pepper, balsamic, spicy red pepper flakes, VODKA and "cream", this sauce is simple to make, but has a complex depth.

Servings:
Yield: 6 cups
Servings: 12
Serving Size: 1/2 cup

R D
1-1

- last checked 11/15/22 -
Use your mobile device's 'Camera' App to look at this code for nutritional info.

Ingredients:

- 4 medium fresh garlic cloves, rough chopped
- 1 medium onion, diced
- 1 tsp salt
- 1/4 tsp cracked black pepper
- 1/4 tsp red pepper flakes
- olive oil cooking spray, 6 second spray ***
- (1) 29-30oz can and (1) 15oz can, crushed tomatoes (45 total).
- 3 oz (1/3 cup) Vodka
- 1/2 cup fresh basil, loosely packed, chopped
- 1-1/2 tsp balsamic vinegar
- 1-1/2 tsp red wine vinegar
- 1 cup unsweetened plain almond milk
- 2 Tbsp reduced fat Parmesan-Style grated topping
  (like the Kraft sprinkles you get at a pizzaria, in a shaker)

Directions:

1. In a medium sized pot, spray the cooking spray over the onions, garlic, salt, pepper and red pepper flakes. Cook until softened, around 6-7 minutes on medium heat.
2. Add the crushed tomatoes, vodka mixture, and vinegars. Cover and allow to cook at a low simmer for 20 minutes.
3. Carefully pour the hot sauce into a food processor, with the fresh chopped basil, then puree until almost smooth. You can also use a blender, in batches.
4. Return the sauce to your pot, add parmesan topping and almond milk. Stir to combine, then cover and simmer for 5 minutes. Done

Notes:

- Big bottles of Vodka are expensive. They sell small $3 bottles at corner liquor stores or at BevMo, any brand works.
- If you can't use almond milk, due to allergies, use soy or cashew milk. Kroger also has an awesome brand of low point, thick milk, called "Carbmaster" that's 1 point per cup. Honestly though, this is so low in points, with so many servings, that you can use whatever you want. Just remember to adjust the points.

White Wine Butter & Garlic Sauce

A delicious herbed garlic butter sauce with a subtle wine taste

Servings Info.:

- Yields: 2 cups
- Servings: 4
- Serving Size: 1/2 cup

R D
1-1

- last checked 11/15/22 -
Use your mobile device's 'Camera' App to
look at this code for nutritional info.

You would be a straight up liar if you said that you didn't love a good white wine butter sauce, but let's see... what's the main problem with that sauce if you're in Weight Watchers? Oh yeah, a giganto amount of points from butter and wine. Here's the deal though, simply follow the ideas in this guide and figure out how to OUT SMART your food. A few simple food swaps, from thinking outside of the box, makes this sauce possible. We up the servings by stretching with water and chicken broth, to lower the points per serving. Ask yourself, do we REALLY need 1/2 cup of white wine in the sauce? Guess what, 3 Tbsp of it, plus 2 Tbsp of white wine vinegar will still give a great wine flavor, just a more subtle one. Do we really need a ton of butter? Nope. Let's use I Can't Believe It's Not Butter Light, along with some butter flavored cooking spray, to impart a buttery flavor at a fraction of the points. But how do we thicken it without a bunch of heavy cream?... Cornstarch. It'll tighten it up for 40 calories and no fat.

Ingredients:

- 6-8 second spray, butter flavored cooking
- spray. ***
- 1-3/4 cup fat free chicken broth
- 3 Tbsp white wine
- 2 Tbsp white wine vinegar
- 1-1/2 Tbsp I can't believe it's not butter Light
- 1 or 2 medium garlic cloves, chopped
- 1 tsp dried parsley or basil
- 4-1/2 tsp cornstarch
- 1/4 tsp salt
- 1/8 tsp pepper

Directions:

1. Combine all of the ingredients in a small sauce pot, whisk to combine.
2. Bring the sauce to a rolling boil over, high heat.
3. Allow the sauce to cook at a rolling boil for 4 minutes.
4. Remove from heat and season with salt and pepper, to taste. It will thicken more as it cools.

Notes:

- If you would like a creamier sauce for no additional points, you can replace 1/4 cup of the water with 1/4 cup of unsweetened almond milk. You can also use 3 Tbsp of fat free/skim milk in place of an equal amount of the water.
- You can add in some red pepper flakes, different herbs than parsley, and some lemon juice, but then you'd be treading on the "Scampi Sauce" recipe's territory.
- This same principle can be used to make a red wine sauce. Replace the chicken broth with beef broth, the white wine with red, use red wine vinegar, remove the parsley and basil, then increase the salt to 1/2 tsp and the black pepper to 1/4 tsp.

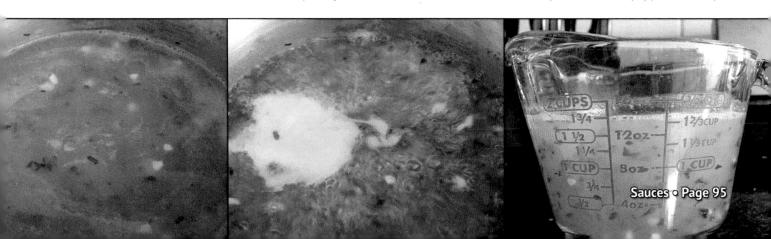

Yum Yum Sauce

A deliciously creamy, savory and slightly spicy cream sauce, perfect for dipping

Yum Yum sauce is an extremely popular sauce, found at Japanese steakhouses and Teppanyaki restaurants. It's a savory, sweet, slightly spicy cream sauce. You'll usually find it served as a dipping sauce for cooked/grilled meats. If you'd like to try a version with a slightly smoky flavor, try replacing the regular paprika with some smoked paprika. A great thing about this sauce is how easy it is to adjust the heat level. As-is, it has a very slight hint of heat. If you like 'a de"spice... go to town with the cayenne.

Ingredients:

- 3/4 cup plain fat free Greek yogurt
- 1 Tbsp light mayonnaise
- 1-1/2 Tbsp rice vinegar
- 2-1/2 Tbsp no sugar added ketchup
- 1 tsp paprika
- 1 tsp garlic powder
- 2 tsp 0 point sugar replacement o' choice
- 1/4 tsp salt
- 1/4 tsp black pepper
- 1 pinch o' cayenne pepper (or more, to taste)

Serving Info:

Yield: 1 cup
Servings: 4
Serving Size: 1/4 cup

RECIPE INFO

R D
0-1

- last checked 11/15/22 -
Use your mobile device's 'Camera' App to
look at this code for nutritional info.

Directions:

1. Add all of the ingredients into a bowl, whisk together till combined. Cover and set aside. It's tasty as is, ,but the flavors develop the longer it sits.
2. Omg... I made a recipe with only 1 step!! Can I get an Amen!!!

Notes:

- If you don't want to use mayonnaise, feel free to replace it with an extra Tablespoon of Greek, it'll still taste great. Plus, it'll remove 1 point from the ingredients.

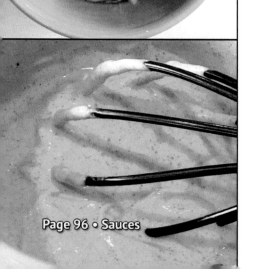

Hummus

My healthier version of on an internationally beloved dip

Traditionally, Hummus is made with garbanzo beans, garlic, lemon juice, tahini (crushed sesame seed paste), and lots and lots and looooooots of extra virgin olive oil. It's usually so high in points and calories that the popular skinny cooking sites, and even the manufacturers, have their serving sizes at a mere 2 tablespoons. Anyone who has ever had hummus knows... 2 Tablespoons is NOT a realistic serving size. I also decided to add a couple of suggestions for how you can easily modify the standard recipe, to make a few popular variations.

LOW POINT HUMMUS

YIELDS: 4 cups
Servings: 16
Serving Size: 1/4 cup

RECIPE INFO

R D
1-1

- last checked 11/15/22 -
Use your mobile device's 'Camera' App to look at this code for nutritional info.

Ingredients:

- (2) 15oz cans of garbanzo beans/chickpeas, drained, reserve liquid. You are left with 17.5oz of actual chickpeas.
- 2 Tbsp tahini (sesame paste)
- 1/4 cup lemon juice
- 4-5 fresh garlic cloves (to taste)
- 1/3 cup reserved garbanzo bean juice
- 2 Tbsp water (or more, if you want it thinner)
- 1/3 cup fat free yogurt (or greek)
- 1 tsp olive oil (get one that says 'robust' or 'bold' flavor)
- 2 tsp ground cumin
- 3/4 tsp salt
- 1/4 tsp sesame oil (adds a nice pop of nuttiness, making up for the lack of additional Tahini)

Directions:

1 Drain the garbanzo beans, reserve the liquid, and rinse off the beans.
2 Add the garbanzo beans, tahini, lemon juice, garlic, garbanzo bean juice, water, yogurt, oils, cumin, and salt to a large blender or food processor and process until pureed and smooth.
3 If the mixture is too thick, add more water into the food processor, 1 Tablespoon at a time, until it takes on a very smooth, creamy and easily spreadable consistency.
4 Garnish with a dusting of paprika and minced parsley. Spray the top of the hummus with a quick touch of olive oil cooking spray.

FLAVORED HUMMUS

You can make a wide range of flavored Hummus, by simply adding a few extra ingredients into the food processor. Here's a small list of ideas.

Roasted Red Pepper Hummus: *(add the following)*

- 1 or 2 roasted red peppers (peel off the skin)
- 2 tsp regular or smoked paprika

Southwest Hummus: *(add the following)*

- 2 canned chipotle peppers in adobo sauce
- 1/2 tsp chili powder
- (optional) replace the lemon juice with lime juice

Sun Dried Tomato & Basil Hummus: *(add the following)*

- 1/2 cup (or more) sundried tomatoes, rinse off the oil.
- 1/4 cup chopped fresh basil

Black Bean Hummus: *(add the following)*

- Use the liquid from the garbanzo bean can, like normal, but...
- Instead of using actual garbanzo beans, use rinsed black beans.
- Yes... open a can of garbanzo beans, save the juice and set the garbanzo beans aside for something else. No whining, just do it!

Pumpkin Hummus: *(add the following)*

- Replace one of the 15oz cans of garbanzo beans, with a 15oz can of pumpkin puree.

Pesto Hummus: *(add the following)*

- 1/2 cup fresh basil
- 1 cup fresh chopped spinach
- 1 Tbsp kraft reduced fat parmesan topping

Closing Thoughts

The Writings of Lord Daniel von Hallakstein

Lord Daniel von Hallakstein VII, Ruler of Gluttonia *(1573-1622)*
Protector of Gluttons, Slayer of Points & Keeper of the Seven Spices

As you've probably realized by now, this isn't a full fledged, stand-alone cookbook. This is a quasi instructional cooking guide, that I want you to use to begin creating. I want to encourage you to use the recipes in here, along with the ideas for ingredient swaps and the recipe builder tutorial, to start playing around with recipes. Open up cookbooks, go online to food websites, look up delicious high calorie dishes, then put them in the builder and start tweakin'.

This book contains everything that you'll need to completely o-freakin-bliterate any feelings of helplessness that you've had with your meals. Is your husband a non-supportive schmo that complains about your "diet cooking?" That doesn't have to be the case anymore. Are you stressing about how much you miss one dish or another? Hack it down. Sub out the Italian sausage for my recipe, replace the the heavy cream with some almond milk and cornstarch... you can do this.

If there is one thing that I would ask of you, it's that you PLEASE share with me your triumphs and setbacks in the kitchen. We're all stronger together and we're all walking the same path. If you use my Recipe Builder tutorial to tweak a recipe to be lower in points and you want to show that baby off? Post it in Connect! Use the hashtag *#RecipeBuilderChallenge*, along with what the original points per servings were, followed by what you lowered it to with your tweaks. After playing with recipes a few times, through trial and error, you'll find techniques that really work for you. Share those in your post so they might help others. Need help with a recipe? Ask! Heck, feel free to submit a question to me directly through *info@theguiltfreegourmet.net*, or shoot me a message on Connect. I'll respond if I see it... and remember. If I don't, I probably missed it, so resend it, I don't mind. Guys are forgetful, it's a curse. 👤

Though this IS a stand alone cooking guide, this book will be **ESSENTIAL** for my upcoming cookbook. Almost every single dish there will reference foundation recipes that are found in this book. In my cookbook, as an example, I can't type out the ingredient lists for all of the foundation recipes, into every Appetizer recipe that calls for them. As an example, on the chorizo stuffed tamale balls, I can't take an entire page to add the recipe for my chorizo, my low point masa & my roasted tomatillo sauce, into that recipe. I will simply make a note that the recipe calls for *"1lb batch of my chorizo, pg # of the cooking guide" "2 cups prepared Masa, pg # of the cooking guide"* etc. Consider this to be the 1st Volume of my cookbook, where the actual main dish recipes begin in volume 2 and reference foundation recipes and sauces in this book. I'd like to combine it all together into one big SUPER BOOK... but it would cost waaaay too much on Amazon.

With that said, thank you so much for your support and enouragement through this entire project. Thank you for allowing me the opportunity to be able to help you in your journey, as well as for helping me be able to feel like I'm helping make a difference. Now that we all have the warm fuzzies goin', remember,

YOU'VE GOT THIS!!!!

Acknowledgements

Well here we are again. When I wrote my acknowledgements for the first edition of this book, back in 2018, I never in a MILLION YEARS would have imagined that it would ever blow up to the point that it has. I started the entire project out of a desire to help folks, but then a crazy thing happened, ya'll ended up helping me just as much. As most of you stay at home parents know, you lose your sense of self and personal worth, when your entire purpose, day in and day out... is to just stay shut in your house, changing diapers and shuttling kids around. Suddenly, this whole book went full-on best seller. In just over 10 months, it was downloaded over 350,000 times and sold over 11,000 copies. I started getting emails from people all across the country, telling me how it had completely changed their lives and given them hope with their weight loss journeys.

I had one sweet lil grandma tell me how she made tamales for the first time in her life, for her picky husband who always picked on her "diet cooking", how much he loved them and how wonderful she felt. A mom sending me a video of her and her young daughter making fresh pasta together for the first time, complete with the adorable little girl narrating "look Daniel, we're doing it!" Pictures of a family sitting around their Christmas dinner table, full of my holiday dishes, all smiling for the camera. A woman who made one of my sugar free cakes for her diabetic father... and on, and on, and on... I cannot even begin to express to you folks how much you have all touched my life and changed me as a person, because of all of this.

I started all of this because all of you, in Connect, badgering me to do it in the Spring of 2017. When I had to resign from my job, to stay home and take care of Jesse and Rachel, I never would have thought that my website and graphics experience would ever be used for anything, ever again, other than maybe getting a tiny side job every now and then... and look where we are now. Folks, this was the perfect storm. There are people in Connect who could haaaaaaands down cook me under the table any day of the week and twice on Sunday. Mappleby777, Longhorn_Sooner, and Hannahamil, just to name a few. There are some fanTASTIC cooks in Connect that you all should definitely be following. I just got lucky because I have experience doing graphics layouts, otherwise we wouldn't be here.

Well, with that lil bit of instrospection out of the way, I'll try to rattle off a few names of people who were very important to this Fourth Edition (2023) getting made. In the first book I named nearly 40-50 people. I can't do that this time, I'd leave too many people out, on accident. I'm following over 4,600 people, so I can't mention all of you, but know that I ONLY click to follow you if you've said or done something that has connected with me personally. So even if you're not mentioned in here, I still thank you.

Thank you, of course, to my wife, who continues to put up with me. My kids, for turning me into a better person, despite all of the stains on my clothes now. And lastly, I'll thank my Mom, who made me first start thinking about the need to modify recipes specifically for people with dietary restrictions. You'll never know what an impact it had on me, that one Thanksgiving... seeing you standing there eating a hamburger patty out of a ziplock bag, from your purse, while all of us were piling our plates high with food... and you couldn't eat any of it because of your heart... and none of us had taken that into consideration. There was nothing you could eat, at Thanksgiving. I'll never get that image out of my mind. I just wish you could have been here long enough for me to cook for you, now that I'm actually good at it. Plus... I'm pretty sure that you would have loved Jesse and Rachel.

Nutritional Values

One of the biggest reasons for cooking and preparing meals like I do, is because I want to eat amazingly snazzy food, without having to reduce my portion sizes. If you look, you'll notice that the serving sizes for all of my sauces, are between 1/4 to 1/2 cup. Most popular 'skinny' and cookbook authors, usually only have a serving size of 1-2 Tablespoons. MINE give you at least double that amount for the same points or less. In equal amounts, my recipes are usually around 1/2 (or less) of the points, fat and calories of everyone else. Seriously, "Eat a responsible 2 Tbsps of sauce..." or "Lightly dip your fork into the full fat, normal sauce, so you won't need as much..." sure sounds like being on a diet to ME. Teach people to cook differently, so that they don't HAVE to feel like they are on a diet. But what do I know... I'm just the guy that lost 53lbs in 3.5 months, eating like this. *#IfEyeRollsCouldBurnCalories.*

MEAT SEASONINGS (with 99% FF ground turkey)	POINTS RANGE 1 serving	SERVING SIZE	CALORIES	FAT (grams)	CARBS (grams)	SUGAR (grams)	PROTEIN (grams)	PAGE #
Andouille	0-0	2oz	101	4.4	2.6	0.2	11	24
Asian	0-0	2oz	100	6	2	1	11	24
Bratwurst	0-0	2oz	80	1	3	1	14	25
Breakfast Sausage	0-0	2oz	70	1	3	2	14	25
Chorizo	0-0	2oz	70	1	2	0	14	26
Cuban Picadillo	0-0	2oz	100	3	4	1	13	26
Greek	0-0	2oz	130	4.3	9	2.3	12	27
Italian Sausage	0-0	2oz	100	4	1	0	12	27
Jerk Seasoning	0-0	2oz	70	1	2	1	14	28
Kielbasa	0-0	2oz	60	1	1	0	14	28
Lebanese Kafta	0-0	2oz	80	1	4	1	14	29
"Savory" Ground Turkey	0-0	2oz	70	1	2	1	14	29
Taco Seasoning	0-0	2oz	92	4.2	1	0.2	11	30
Texas Hot Link	0-0	2oz	70	1	1	0.2	11	30

FOUNDATIONS	POINTS RANGE	SERVING SIZE	CALORIES	FAT (grams)	CARBS (grams)	SUGAR (grams)	PROTEIN (grams)	PAGE #
2 Ingredient Dough	13-13	1 cup ball	180	0	32	20	12	32-33
2 ID: 1/2 section	7-7	1/2 cup ball	90	0	16	10	6	--
2 ID: 1/4 section	3-3	1/4 cup ball	45	0	8	5	3	--
2 ID: 1/8 section	2-2	1/8 cup ball	22.5	0	4	2.5	1.5	--
Breading 1.0	1	1/4 cup	25	1	10	0	3	34
Breading 2.0	1	1/4 batch	80	2.5	9	1	4	35
Cream Cheese Substitute	0-7	(full batch)	531	3.5	32.5	29.3	92.1	36
Masa	1-2	1/16 section	473	0	96	8	23.5	38-39
Fresh Pasta	3-3	1/4 cup ball	168	3.85	24	0.2	8	40
Pie Crust	1-1	1/8	50	0	26	6	2	44
Pudding Hack	n/a	n/a	--	--	--	--	--	45
Ricotta Gnocchi	4-4	1/4 section	70	0.5	12	0	2	42
Roasted Garlic	n/a	n/a	--	--	--	--	--	46
Toasted Spices	n/a	n/a	--	--	--	--	--	47
Slider Pretzel Buns	2-2	1/8 bun	25	1	3	2	1	48
Yeast Burger Buns	3-3**	1 bun	100	0.5	21	2.4	11	50
Yeast Pizza Dough	15-15	Entire Crust	490	1.5	102	4	15	52

POINTS:

Remember everyone, the listed values for each recipe only show the points for ONE SERVING. A lot of my sauces stay 0 or 1 point for 2,3,4 or even 5 servings. To find out the accurate values for multiple servings, please go to my website, look in the "nutritional values" page, and click the appropriate recipe to open it up in your own App. Then, you'll be able to scroll up and down to find the info. for multiple servings, as well as being able to track your food through the app.

SAUCES	POINT RANGE 1 serving	SERVING SIZE	CALORIES	FAT (grams)	CARBS (grams)	SUGAR (grams)	PROTEIN (grams)	PAGE #
Arrabbiata	0-0	1 cup	63	1.8	9.4	5	1.7	56
Alfredo	1-1	1/4 cup	50	1	9	2	2	63
Asian Dipping/Glaze	0-0	1/4 cup	15	0	7	2	1	57
Avocado Cilantro	1-1	1/4 cup	60	2.5	7	5	2	58
Bang Bang	0-1	1/4 cup	46	1.1	3.7	2.6	4.8	59
Barbecue (BBQ)	0-0	1/2 cup	25	0	6	3	1	60
Bearnaise	0-0	1/4 cup	45	3	2	0	1	61
Bechamel	0-1	1/4 cup	40	0	8	2	1	62
Black Peppercorn	1-1	1/2 cup	20	0.5	3	1	1	64
Bolognese	0-0	1/2 cup	100	3.5	8	4	9	65
Buffalo	0-0	1/4 cup	10	0.5	2	0	0	66
Butter	1-1	1/4 cup	30	2.5	1	0	0	67
Cheese	1-1	1/4 cup	15	0	3	0	0	68
Chimichurri	1-1	1/4 cup	54	4.6	3	0.3	1	69
Cilantro Lime	0-0	1/4 cup	20	1	2	0	0	70
Clam	1-1	1/2 cup	40	0.5	5	1	1	71
Country Gravy with Sausage	1-1	1/2 cup	140	3	10	4	19	72
Creamy Herb	0-1	1/4 cup	40	0	8	2	1	63
Creamy Horseradish	0-1	1/4 cup	40	0.6	3.8	2.9	5.1	73
Curry Cream	0-0	1/2 cup	34	0.9	4.7	1	2	74
Florentine	1-1	1/2 cup	70	0	13	3	3	75
Gravy	0-0	1/4 cup	10	0	1	0	1	76
Hollandaise	1-1	1/4 cup	170	13	3	0	8	77
Katsu	1-1	1/4 cup	105	0.1	22.1	19.3	1.6	78
Korean Gochujang	1-1	1/4 cup	77	0.2	16.5	11.3	1.2	79
Lemon & Chive	0-1	1/4 cup	45	0	9	2	1	63
Marinara	0-0	1/2 cup	40	0.5	5	2	1	80
Marsala	1-1	3/4 cup	65	0.5	9.1	2.5	3.9	81
Mexican Brown Mole'	1-1	1/2 cup	70	3	14	6	4	82
Parmesan Pomodoro	0-0	1/2 cup	40	0.7	8.1	5	1.	83
Pesto	1-1	1/4 cup	45	3	2	0	2	84
Piccata	1-1	1/2 cup	25	1	3	0	0	85
Pineapple Chili	0-1	1/4 cup	29	0.1	7.6	5.5	0.4	86
Red Enchilada	0-0	1/2 cup	45	0.5	9	5	2	87
Roasted Red Pepper Marinara	0-0	1/2 cup	50	1	8	5	1	88
Roasted Tomatillo	0-0	1/2 cup	60	1	11	6	2	89
Roasted Garlic Cream	1-1	1/4 cup	50	0.5	9	2	1	63
Scampi (calculated WITH shrimp)	1-1	1/2 cup	220	3	10	0	35	90
Steak Sauce (A2)	1-1	1/4 cup	44	0.2	8.6	6.6	0.7	91
Teriyaki	0-0	1/4 cup	14	0.1	10.3	7.8	0.8	92
Tzatziki	0-1	1/4 cup	41	1.1	3	2	5.1	93
Vodka	1-1	1/2 cup	50	0.5	9	5	2	94
White Wine Butter Sauce	1-1	1/2 cup	25	1	1	0	0	95
Yum Yum	0-1	1/4 cup	52	1.4	6.7	5.2	4.9	96
** Hummus (regular)	1-1	1/4 cup	70	2.5	9	2	3	97

PLEEEEEEASE LEAVE A REVIEW ON AMAZON

If you found the info/recipes in this book helpful, PLEASE pay it back by leaving a review, folks.
I'm self published, so every review counts. Though LOTS of people bought this cookbook in 2022,
only 3 people have left a review on Amazon this ENTIRE YEAR (as of 11/15/2022). C'mon peeps, help a guy out lol.

Book Index

Daniel Bonaparte - Emperor of France 1769-1821

Might I recommend the Bechamel sauce? Viva la France!

Made in the USA
Middletown, DE
31 March 2023

27995182R00058